The flowering plants of South Africa vol. 4

By

I. B. Pole Evans

PUBLISHED BY: 2024 by BTB Publishing

ISBN : 978-1-63652-371-2

THE FLOWERING PLANTS OF SOUTH AFRICA

VOL. 4

I. B. POLE EVANS

CONTENTS

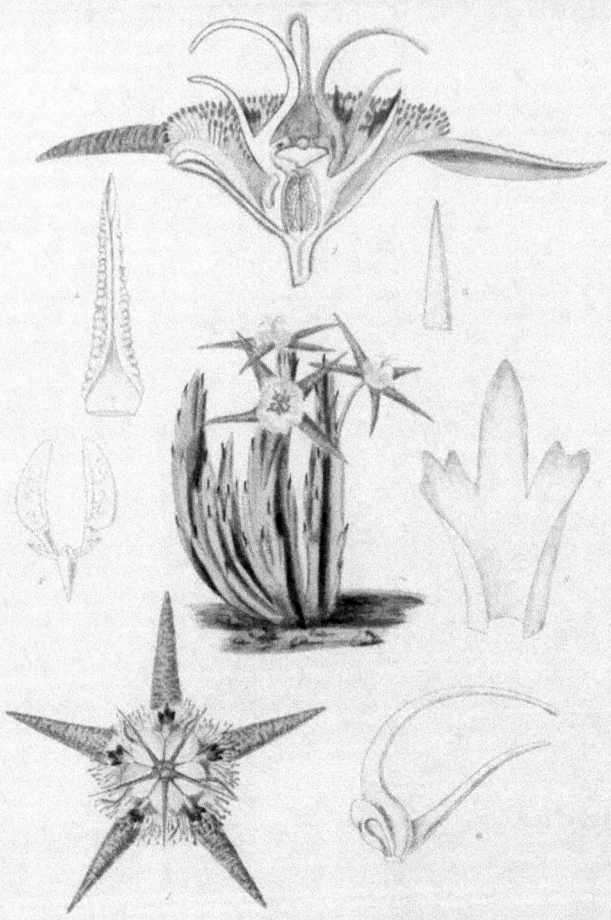

PLATE 121.

STAPELIA FLAVOPURPUREA.
Cape Province.

ASCLEPIADACEAE. *Tribe* STAPELIEAE.

STAPELIA, *Linn.; Benth. et Hook. f. Gen. Plant.*
Stapelia flavopurpurea, *Marloth in Trans. S. Afr. Phil. Soc.*

Representatives of this characteristic South African genus have been figured on Plates 26 and 72, and we have pleasure in illustrating for the first time in colour a species which is unique among the species of *Stapelia*. It differs from all the known species in having clavate hairs on the disc. The flowers, though much smaller than many in the genus, are very beautiful, and lack the unpleasant smell so characteristic of stapelias.

It is not a common species, and as far as our records go has only been collected in the Tanqua Karroo by Dr. Marloth, and recently the Division of Botany received specimens from Mr. E. Anderson, Matjesfontein. This flowered at Pretoria in February 1923, and our Plate was prepared from these specimens.

DESCRIPTION:—*Stems* 4 cm. high, 4-angled, minutely pubescent. *Rudimentary leaves* 2 mm. long, deltoid, acute. *Flowers* 1-3 together arising about 2/3 up the stem. *Pedicels* 1·7 cm. long, terete, minutely pubescent. *Sepals* 5 mm. long, linear-lanceolate, acute, minutely pubescent. *Corolla* 3·6 cm. across when expanded; lobes 1·5 cm. long, ovate-lanceolate, strongly revolute, so that they appear almost linear, acute, strongly rugose; tube saucer-shaped, covered with numerous clavate hairs about 1 mm. long. *Outer corona lobes* 4Â·5 mm. long, 3-lobed, concave on the inner face, with the middle lobe narrower and longer than the side lobes and with the side lobes sometimes bifid or trifid. *Inner corona lobes* 5 mm. long, incumbent over the anthers, 2-horned, with the upper horn erect and curving outwards above, and with the lower horn erect-spreading shorter than the upper horn (National Herb. 2712).

PLATE 121.—Fig. 1, surface view of flower; Fig. 2, median longitudinal section of flower; Fig. 3, sepal; Fig. 4, petal; Fig. 5, outer corona; Fig. 6, inner corona and pollen sac; Fig. 7, pollinia.

F.P.S.A., 1924.

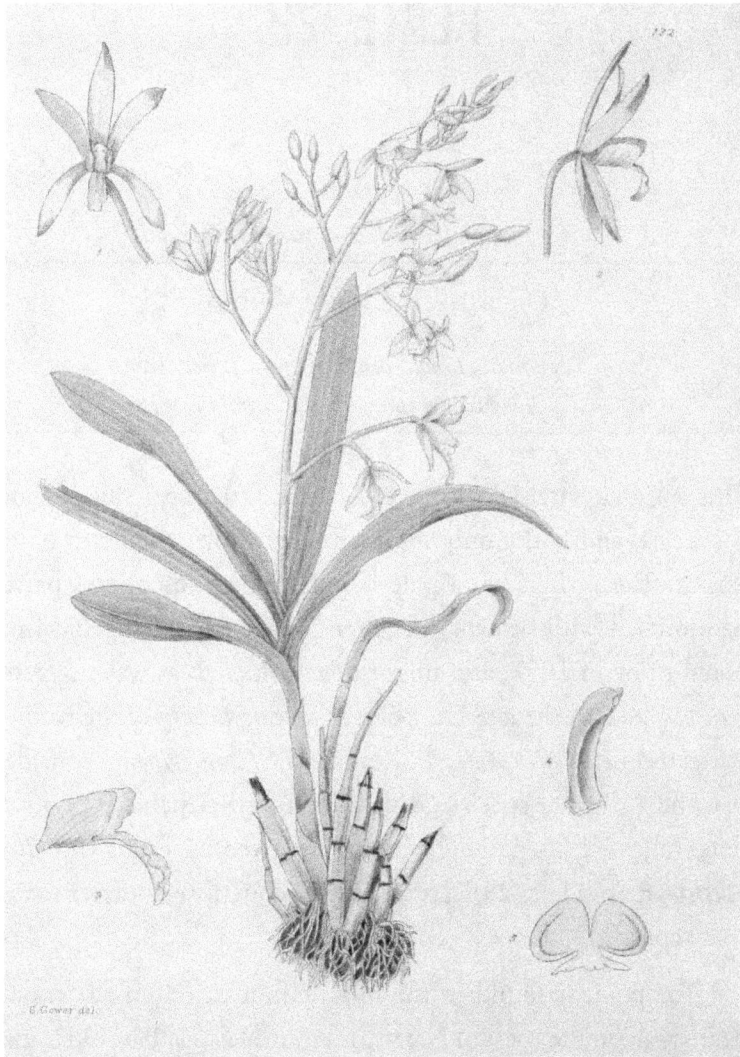

PLATE 122.

ANSELLIA GIGANTEA.
Transvaal, Natal, Portuguese East Africa.

ORCHIDACEAE. *Tribe* VANDEAE.

ANSELLIA, *Lindl.*; *Benth. et Hook. f. Gen. Plant.*
Ansellia gigantea, *Reichb. f. in Linnaea.*

This epiphytic orchid belongs to a tropical African genus of about 6 species, and is the only representative which occurs in South Africa. The flowers are a pale lemon colour, sometimes barred or blotched with brown. Specimens were sent to England from Natal prior to 1857, and might be considered, as was suggested by Hooker and the late Dr. Bolus, a colour variety of the tropical African *Ansellia africana*. Mr. Rolfe in the *Flora Capensis* considers it to be a distinct species, as described by Reichenbach, and we have followed his naming. The figure given by Bolus (*Ic. Orch. Austro-Afric.* 11. t. 29) represents a colour form different from that reproduced here.

The plant is found in the mountainous parts of the eastern Transvaal, on the coast of Natal, and near Delagoa Bay. Our figure was prepared from a specimen which flowered at the Division of Botany in June 1922, and which was collected by Mrs. Sinclair Allen on the Lebombo Mountains in Swaziland.

DESCRIPTION:—*Stems* elongate, terete or somewhat sulcate, 1/3-1 ft. long, with 6 to many leaves on the upper part or near the apex and numerous imbricate membranous sheaths below. *Leaves* distichous, linear-oblong to elliptic-lanceolate, subacute, Â¼-1 ft. long, Â½-1Â½ in. broad, with 3-5 prominent veins. *Panicle* terminal, Â½-1 ft. long, usually with several branches, rarely reduced to a simple raceme, with a few short sheaths below. *Bracts* triangular-ovate, subacute, 1/6 in. long. *Pedicels* slender, 1-1Â¼ in. long. *Flowers* medium-sized, light yellow, more or less barred or blotched with light dusky brown; sepals and petals spreading, oblong or elliptic-oblong, obtuse, about Â¾ in. long; lip 3-lobed, rather shorter than the sepals; side lobes erect, oblong, obtuse; front lobe recurved, elliptic-oblong, obtuse or emarginate; disc with 3 prominent crenulate keels; column clavate, 1/3 in. long (National Herb. Pretoria 2601).

PLATE 122.—Figs. 1, 2, front and side view of flower; Fig. 3, lip; Fig. 4, column; Fig. 5, pollinia.

F.P.S.A., 1924.

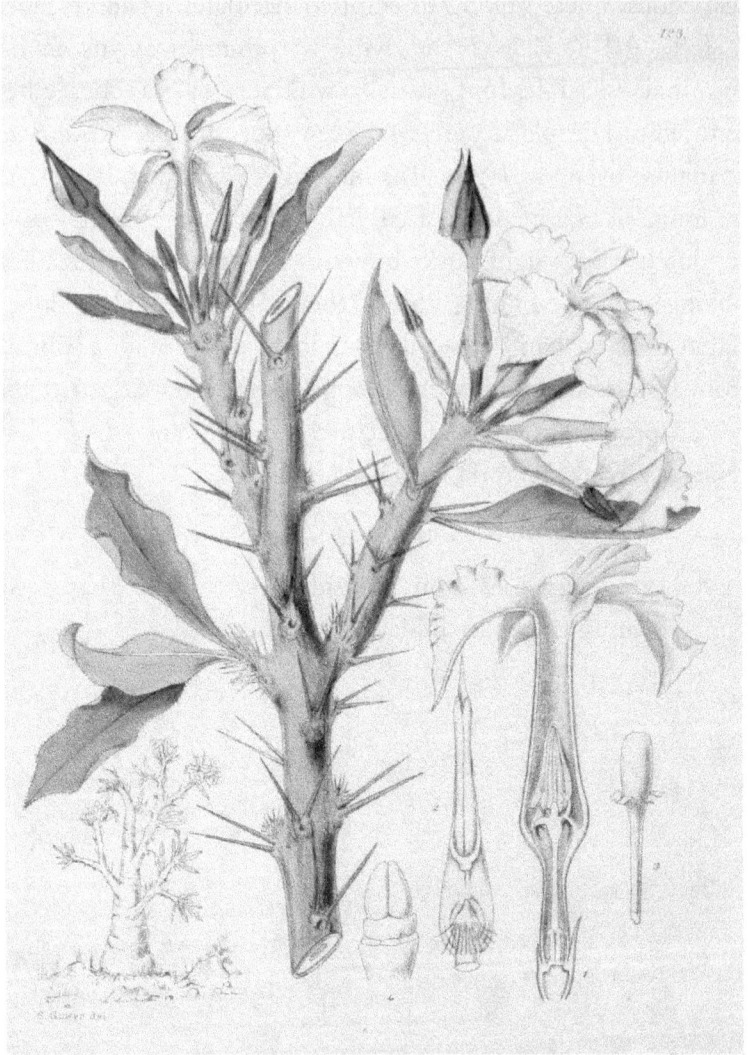

PLATE 123.

PACHYPODIUM SAUNDERSII.
Transvaal, Swaziland.

APOCYNACEAE. *Tribe* ECHITIDEAE.

PACHYPODIUM, *Lindl.; Benth. et Hook. f. Gen. Plant.*
Pachypodium Saundersii, N. E. Br. in Kew Bulletin 1892, 126; Fl.

It is with pleasure that we figure for the first time this species of *Pachypodium*, which flowered at the Division of Botany, Pretoria, in 1923, from tubers forwarded by Mr. J. Kirton, Pietersburg, Transvaal. The genus *Pachypodium* differs from *Adenium* (see Plate 16) in having a pair of spines at the base of the leaves, but the present species agrees with *Adenium multiflorum* in its general habit. Both have large succulent stems, partly below the ground, from which the branches arise. In *Pachypodium Saundersii* the pollination mechanism is somewhat complicated, but in what way the various structures function in this is not quite clear. The flowers are protandrous and the anthers all converge to a point. The base of the anther is provided with a pouch and the filament with a ciliated hood, and these two structures form a cage for the pollen. The stigma lies within this cage, and the style may possibly elongate eventually, and thus push the pollen above the anthers, as in the *Compositae*. The plant flowered freely in Pretoria, but failed to fruit, and from this it may be assumed that self-pollination does not take place.

DESCRIPTION:—*Inflorescence* arising in an umbellate manner at apex of stems, up to 11-flowered. *Sepals* 4 mm. long, 3Â·5 mm.

broad, ovate, acuminate, acute, glabrous. *Corolla-tube* 3Â·5 cm. long, cylindric and 1Â·2 cm. long below, with a subglobose base, then suddenly dilated and narrowed towards the apex, glabrous without, pilose within; lobes 2Â·2 cm. long, 1Â·8 cm. broad in the widest part, straight on one side, very convex and crisped on opposite side, subacuminate, acute. *Filament* 3 mm. long, 2 mm. broad, ovate, with a ciliated hood at the base; anthers 6Â·7 mm. long, linear with a lanceolate, acute appendage 1Â·5 mm. long, and a membranous pouch at the base. *Style* 1Â·3 cm. long, terete, glabrous; stigma club-shaped covered with a white opaque jelly-like substance; ovary 3Â·5 mm. long, with a cupular disk at the base (National Herb. 2736).

PLATE 123.—Fig. 1, median longitudinal section of the flower; Fig. 2, stamen; Fig. 3, portion of style with the stigma; Fig. 4, the 2 carpels with a cupular disk at the base.

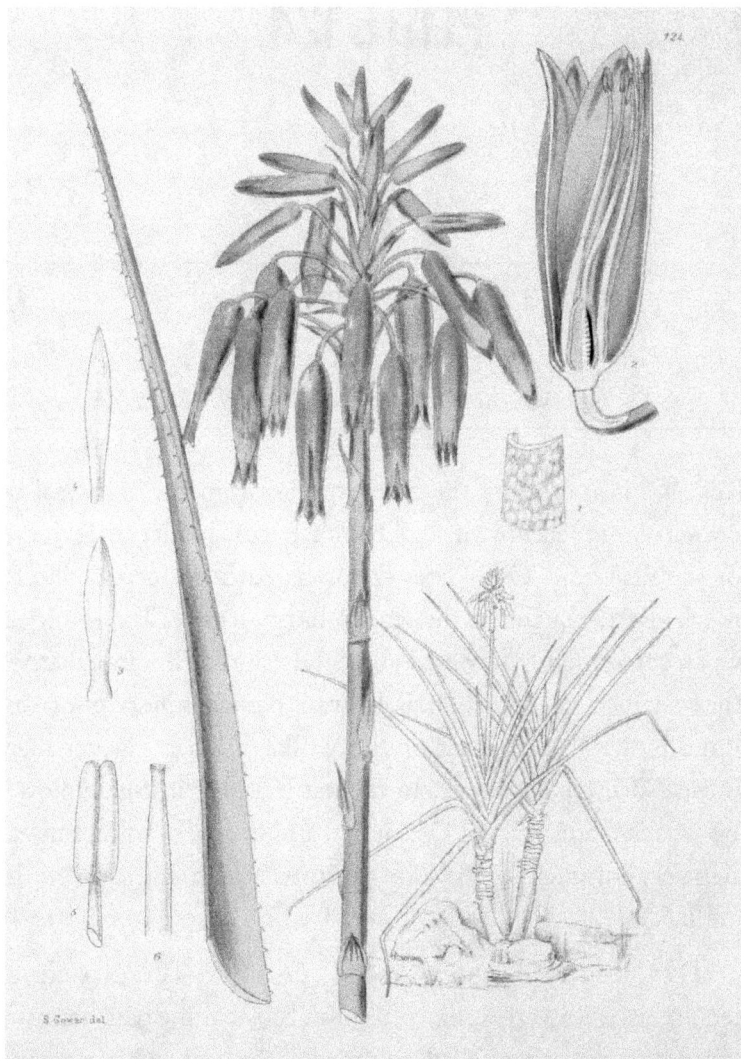

PLATE 124.

ALOE VERECUNDA.
Transvaal.

Liliaceae. *Tribe* Aloineae.

Aloe, *Linn.; Benth. et Hook. f. Gen. Plant.*
Aloe verecunda, *Pole Evans in Trans. Roy. Soc. S. Afr.*

This *Aloe* is another of the many species from the Transvaal described within recent years by Dr. Pole Evans, and it is here figured for the first time. Our Plate was prepared from plants collected by Mr. D. J. Fouche in the Middleburg District, Transvaal, and which subsequently flowered at the Division of Botany, Pretoria. The specimens on which Dr. Pole Evans based his description were found by Mr. P. J. Pienaar on the Wolkberg, near Haenertsberg, in the Northern Transvaal. In the natural state it usually flowers towards the latter part of December, and the dark red racemes are then very conspicuous. As soon as winter sets in, the leaves wither and fall.

Description:—*Stem* short. *Leaves* 8-10, distichous, deciduous, 25-35 cm. long, 8-10 mm. broad at the base, narrowly linear, distinctly channelled, rounded at the back, with numerous minute raised white spots at the base, armed along the edges with delicate white teeth 2-7 mm. apart. *Peduncle* stout, 25 cm. long, clothed with broad ovate shortly cuspidate green empty bracts. *Raceme* more or less capitate. *Bracts* 20 mm. long, 15 mm. broad, ovate, acute. *Pedicels* 25 mm. long. *Perianth* peach-red to scarlet, greenish towards the apex, 26-30 mm. long, 12 mm. in diameter, straight, very markedly 3-angled, contracted towards the mouth; segments free. *Style* and *stamens* not or scarcely exserted (National Herb. 2743).

PLATE 124.—Fig. 1, portion of leaf showing white spots; Fig. 2, median longitudinal section of the flower; Fig. 3, outer perianth-segment; Fig. 4, inner perianth-segment; Fig. 5, anther with part of the filament; Fig. 6, top of style showing the simple stigma.

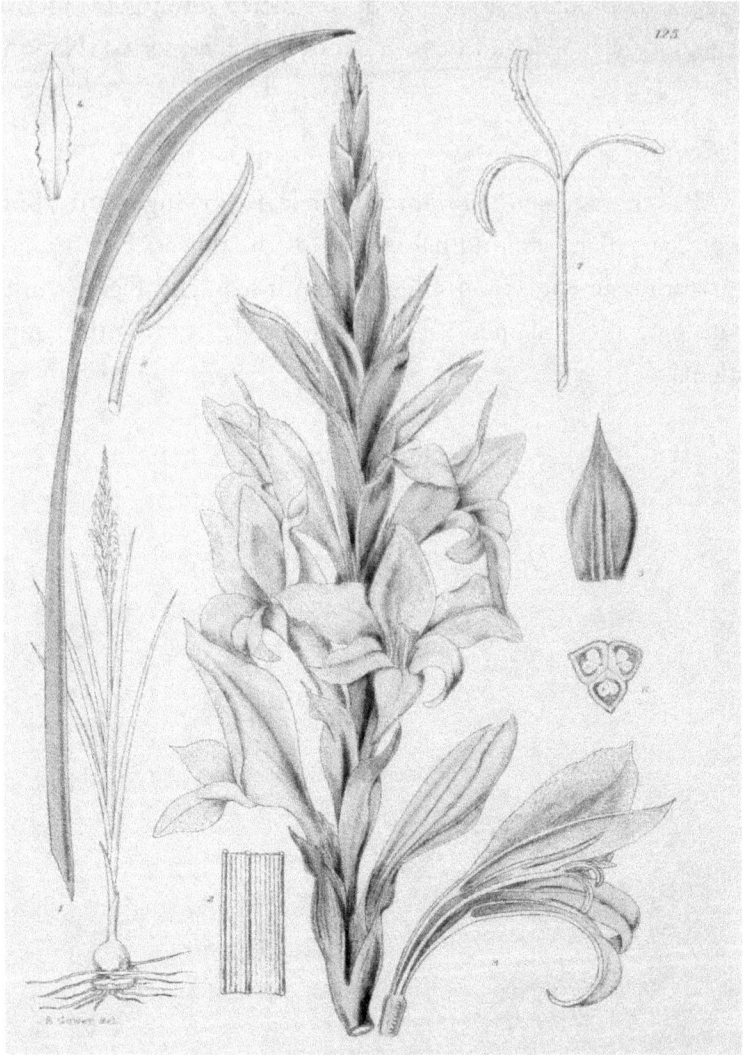

PLATE 125.

GLADIOLUS LUDWIGII var. CALVATUS.
Transvaal.

IRIDACEAE. *Tribe* GLADIOLEAE.

GLADIOLUS, *Linn.*; *Benth. et Hook. f. Gen. Plant.*
Gladiolus Ludwigii, *Pappe. var. calvatus, Baker Fl. Cap.*

This *Gladiolus* belongs to the same section of the genus as *G. Rehmanni*, figured on Plate 20. The variety *calvatus* has up to the present only been recorded from the Pretoria and Barberton Districts of the Transvaal, but the species is a native of Natal, East Griqualand and the Transkei. The specimens from which our illustration was made were collected by Dr. I. B. Pole Evans, C.M.G., at Brits, and were found growing in deep black turf soil. The variety is also figured in the *Botanical Magazine*, t. 6291, and a comparison of that plate with the one reproduced here will show a difference in the colouring of the flowers, but Dr. Pole Evans states that the pale yellow and speckled forms grow together and are undoubtedly the same. The yellow-flowered form was introduced into cultivation in England in 1877, and both this and our plant differ from the species in being glabrous.

DESCRIPTION:—*Plant* about 1 m. high. *Old corm* 4 cm. in diameter, 1Â·5 cm. thick, disc-like; new corm more or less globose on the old corm. *Produced leaves* about 5, the longest up to almost 1 m. long, the free portion of uppermost leaf about 30 cm. long; all 0Â·8-1Â·8 cm. broad, strap-shaped, narrowing to the apex, acute or obtuse, equitant at the base, 12-15-nerved with the main nerves subprominent and with cartilaginous margins, glabrous. *Inflorescence* densely many-flowered, almost 30 cm. long. *Outer spathe valve* 3Â·7 cm. long, 2 cm. broad, ovate, acuminate, acute, 3-keeled below, with membranous margins, glabrous; inner spathe-valve very similar to the outer, but strongly 2-keeled. *Perianth-tube* 1Â·5 cm. long, slightly curved; the upper perianth-lobe 4Â·2 cm. long, 1Â·8 cm. broad, elliptic, shortly apiculate; two upper lateral lobes 3Â·5 cm. long, 2 cm. broad, ovate-elliptic, shortly apiculate at the apex; lowermost lobe 3Â·2 cm. long, 1Â·3 cm. broad, elliptic-ovate, minutely apiculate; two lower lateral lobes 2Â·5 cm. long, 6 mm. broad, linear-oblong, apiculate. *Filaments* 1Â·2 cm. long, terete, glabrous; anthers 1Â·25 cm. long, linear, somewhat sagittate at the base. *Style* 2Â·5 cm. long, terete, glabrous; stigmas 8 mm. long, linear, broadening to the apex (National Herb. 2731).

PLATE 125.—Fig. 1, leaf; Fig. 2, portion of leaf showing ribs; Fig. 3, median longitudinal section of flower; Fig. 4, inner spathe-valve; Fig. 5, outer spathe-valve; Fig. 6, cross-section of ovary; Fig. 7, style and stigmas; Fig. 8, stamen.

F.P.S.A., 1924.

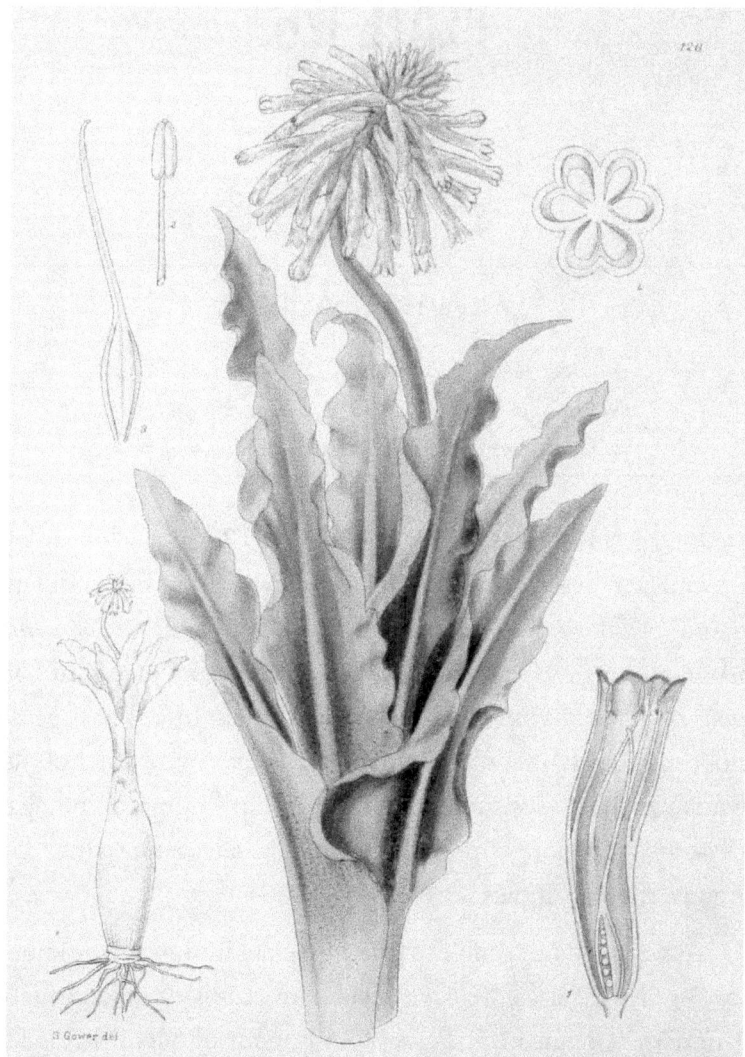

PLATE 126.

VELTHEIMIA ROODEAE.

Cape Province.

LILIACEAE. *Tribe* SCILLEAE.

VELTHEIMIA, *Gled.*; *Benth. et Hook. f. Gen. Plant.*
Veltheimia Roodeae, *Phillips, sp. nov., a V. glauca, Jacq.*
foliis ovatis acuminatis et marginibus undulatis differt.

Bulbus 13 cm. longus, 6 cm. latus. *Folia* 12-15 cm. longa, basi 4-5 cm. lata, ovata, acuminata, apice acuta, marginibus undulatis, glabra. *Pedunculus* 12-15 cm. longus, 6 mm. latus. *Inflorescentia* 3Â·5 cm. longa. *Bracteae* 1 cm. longae. *Pedicellus* 1Â·5 mm. longus. *Tubus perianthii* 2Â·2 cm. longus, cylindricus, basi paullo globosus; lobi 1Â·5 mm. longi, 1Â·5 mm. lati, ovati, apice obtusi. *Filamenta* 1 cm. longa; antherae 2Â·25 mm. longae, oblongae. *Ovarium* 1 cm. longum, 2Â·5 mm. latum, sulcatum; stylus 1 cm. longus; stigma simplex.

As we find it impossible to place this plant into any of the known species of the genus, we have decided to publish a description of it under the name of *V. Roodeae*, in honour of Mrs. R. Rood of Van Rhynsdorp, to whom our readers are greatly indebted for so many of the rare plants we have previously figured. It differs in the shape of the leaves from any of the species described in the *Flora Capensis*. They are distinctly undulate.

Veltheimia is a small genus of 3 species, none of which appears to have been extensively gathered by recent botanical collectors.

The first known species, *V. viridifolia*, was described by Linneaus (as *Aletris capensis*) in 1751, and was introduced into European cultivation in 1768, so that a species of the genus was known to botanical science over 150 years ago.

V. viridifolia, Jacq., does quite well under cultivation, but we have not yet had an opportunity of growing the species here described.

DESCRIPTION:—Bulb 13 cm. long, 6 cm. in diameter, ellipsoid, covered with membranous tunics, at the base with a disc-shaped rootstock 6 cm. in diameter, 2Â·5 cm. thick, from which the roots arise. *Leaves* 11 to a bulb, 12-15 cm. long, 4Â·5 cm. broad near the base, ovate, acuminate, acute, clasping at the base, with undulate margins and a broad thick midrib beneath slightly raised, green and glaucous above, densely reddish-spotted beneath, glabrous. *Peduncle* as long as the leaves, 6 mm. in diameter, terete, reddish by being covered with close-set reddish spots. *Inflorescence* 3Â·5 cm. long. *Bracts* 1 cm. long, almost filiform. *Pedicels* 1Â·5 mm. long. *Flowers* somewhat reflexed; perianth-tube 2Â·2 cm. long, 4 mm. in diameter, cylindric, faintly globose and bent about the middle, white with reddish spots; lobes 1Â·5 mm. long, 1Â·5 mm. broad, ovate, obtuse. *Stamens* fixed to the middle of the perianth-tube; filaments 1 cm. long; anthers 2Â·25 mm. long, oblong. *Ovary* 1 cm. long, 2Â·5 mm. in diameter, in the middle spindle-shaped, furrowed; style 1 cm. long, terete; stigma simple (National Herb. 2739).

PLATE 126.—Fig. 1, median longitudinal section of a flower; Fig. 2, stamen; Fig. 3, pistil; Fig. 4, cross-section through the ovary.

F.P.S.A., 1924.

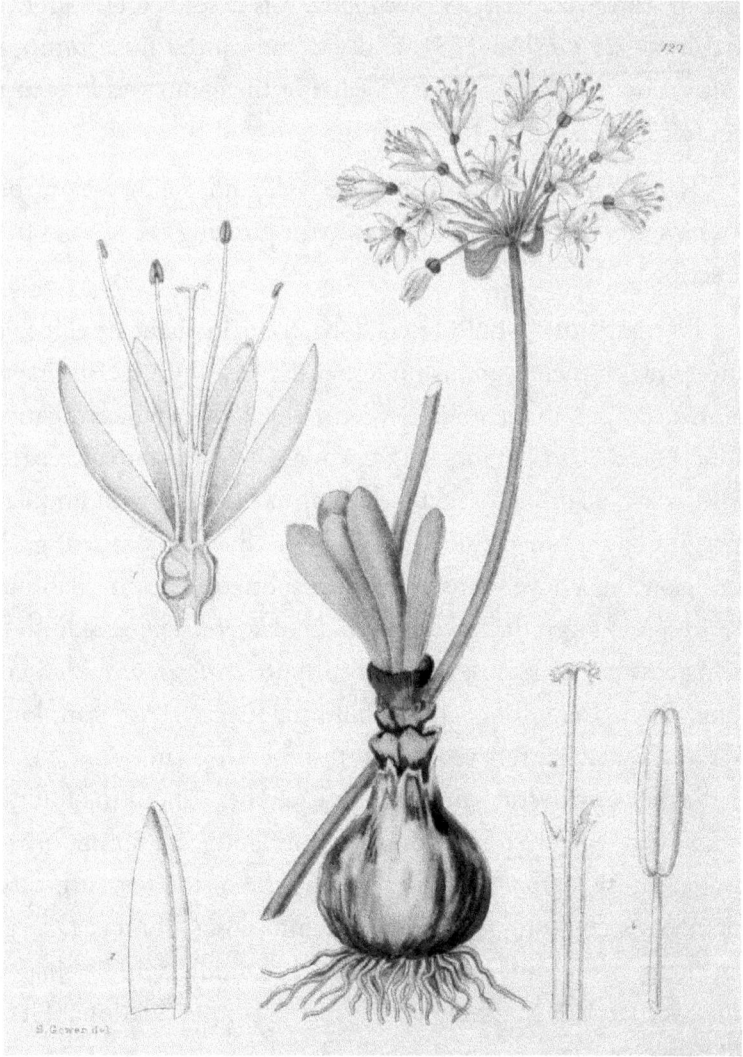

PLATE 127.

STRUMARIA TRUNCATA.

Cape Province.

AMARYLLIDACEAE. *Tribe* AMARYLLEAE.

STRUMARIA, *Jacq.*; *Benth. et Hook. f. Gen. Plant.*
Strumaria truncata, *Jacq. Ic. ii. t. 357; Fl. Cap.*

Strumaria is a small endemic South African genus, and five species have been described in the *Flora Capensis*, all of which have been figured by Jacquin in his *Icones Plantarum Rariorum.* Two of the species are recorded from Little Namaqualand, but no locality is known for the other three, nor do any specimens appear to exist in herbaria, Jacquinâ€™s figures and descriptions being all we know about them. It is with particular pleasure, therefore, that we reproduce this illustration of a species of this little-known genus, and our readers are again indebted to Mrs. E. Rood of Van Rhynsdorp for sending us fresh material. Our plant differs slightly from Jacquinâ€™s figure, inasmuch as the dilated portion of the style does not narrow towards the base and is irregularly lobed above, but on this account we do not feel justified in keeping it distinct from *Strumaria truncata.*

Strumaria truncata is a charming little plant with an umbel of white, sweet-smelling flowers, faintly tinged with pink (the *Flora Capensis* states flowers â€œinodorousâ€). The bulbs received from Mrs. Rood are being grown at the Division of Botany, Pretoria, and we feel sure once the species becomes known it will be sought after by cultivators of our South African bulbs.

DESCRIPTION:—*Bulb* 3 cm. in diameter, globose or ovoid, covered with pale brown papery tunics, and produced into a distinct neck up to 3Â·5 cm. long. *Leaves* 4-6, arising from a sheath, 2Â·2-4Â·5 cm. long, 1Â·2 cm. broad, oblanceolate or oblong (strap-shaped), rounded at the apex, glabrous. *Leaf-sheath* 1Â·5-2 cm. in diameter, funnel-shaped, truncate, fleshy, reddish. *Peduncle* lateral, 15-23 cm. long, terete, glabrous. *Spathe-valves* reddish, 2-3Â·2 cm. long, longer or shorter than the pedicels. *Pedicels* slender, 1Â·2-2 cm. long, glabrous. *Inflorescence* 13-25-flowered; flowers white, faintly but sweet-scented. *Segments* 1 cm. long, 3Â·6 mm. broad, lanceolate, obtuse. *Filaments* connate into a tube for 5 mm., then free for 7 mm., erect, glabrous; anthers 2Â·5 mm. long, oblong, versatile. *Ovary* 1Â·5 mm. long, globose, glabrous, with about 5 ovules in each cell; style dilated, sharply 3-angled below and united with filaments; free part of style 5Â·5 mm. long, terete; stigma minutely 3-fid (National Herb., Pretoria, 2729).

PLATE 127.—Fig. 1, median longitudinal section of the flower; Fig. 2, a perianth segment; Fig. 3, style, showing the dilated 3-angled lower portion of the 3 stigmas; Fig. 4, a stamen.

F.P.S.A., 1924.

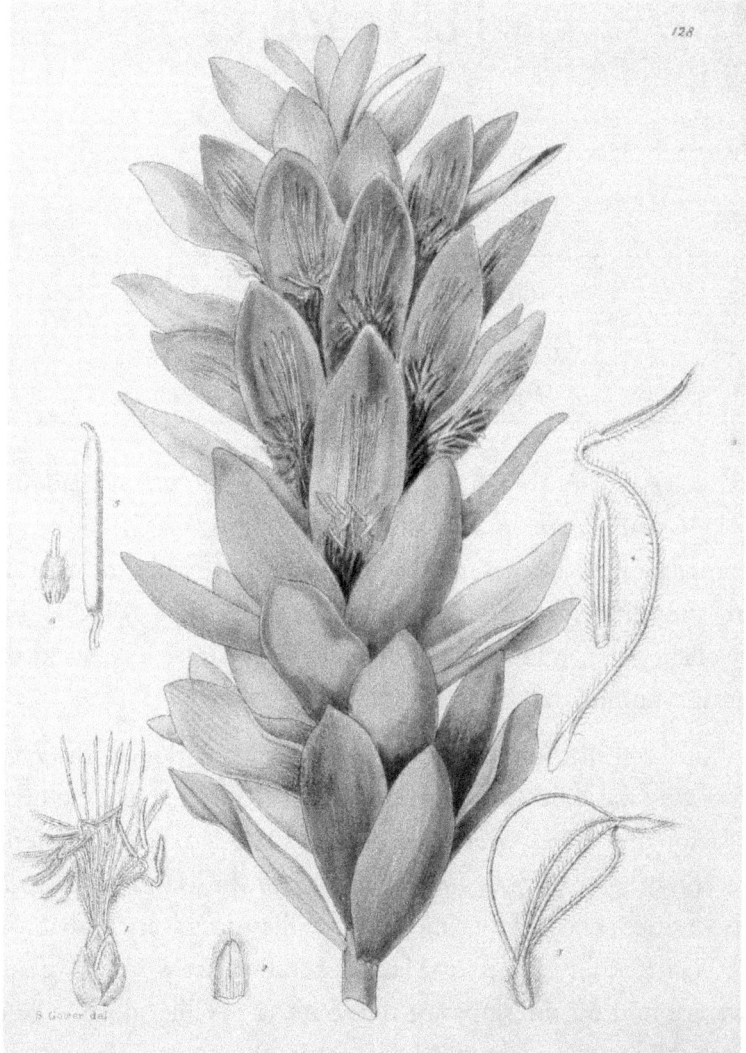

PLATE 128.

MIMETES ARGENTEA.
Cape Province.

PROTEACEAE. *Tribe* PROTEEAE.

MIMETES, *Salisb.*; *Benth. et Hook. f. Gen. Plant.*
Mimetes argentea, Knight, Prot. 67; Fl. Cap.

We have previously figured species of *Mimetes*, viz. *M. palustris* (Pl. 36), *M. hottentotica* (Pl. 82) and *M. capitulata* (Pl. 58), and a comparison of the present Plate with the above will show that *M. argentea* differs from the former two species in the cylindric, not swollen, stigma, and from the latter in the larger leaves and the greater number of flowers in each head.

M. argentea, up to the time of the publication of the *Flora Capensis*, was only known from specimens collected by Roxburgh, Masson and Niven over one hundred years ago, and it was only recently that the species was rediscovered. In May 1923, Mr. A. T. Prentice collected specimens near Villiersdorp, very probably in the same locality visited by Masson. Mr. Prentice writes: â€œThey were found on the slopes of the south (*i.e.* Villiersdorp) side of French Hoek Peak about 3000 ft. There were about 50 trees, 3-6 ft. high, and the habit is different from most of the *Proteaceae* I have noticed. I do not know how to describe it, but it is very open and something like a candelabra, branching all round. The flower spikes all stick straight up, in fact it grows like the advertised type of pruned apple-tree.â€ Mr. R. Hallack came across the species on the Hottentot Holland Mountains, and in June last Mr. T.

P. Stokoe also collected it on the same mountain range. He had noted the plant two years previously, but was unable to obtain it in flower. It is from specimens forwarded by Mr. Stokoe that the present Plate was prepared.

DESCRIPTION:—*Shrub* 4 ft. high; branches velvety-tomentose. *Leaves* 1Â½-2Â½ in. long, 1-1Â½ in. broad, elliptic or oblong-elliptic, with a subobtuse callus at the apex, entire, slightly narrowed to the base, indistinctly 9-nerved, very densely tomentose with adpressed silky hairs. *Heads* subsessile, 1Â½ in. long, including the styles, 7-9-flowered, axillary; involucral bracts about 3-seriate, coriaceous, the outer ovate-oblong, silky tomentose, the inner linear, long-villous; receptacle densely setose with long weak hairs. *Perianth-tube* very short, rusty-villous; segments 1 in. long, linear, rusty-villous; limb 4Â½ in. long, villous. *Stamens* 3 in. long; filaments swollen, fused with the perianth anthers 2Â¾ in. long, linear; apical gland 1/8 in. long, ovoid, acute. *Hypogynous scales* 1Â¼ in. long, linear, subacute, white. *Ovary* Â¾ in. long, oblong, pubescent; style 1Â½ in. long, filiform, glabrous; stigma 3 in. long, linear, obtuse, furrowed, kneed at the junction with the style (National Herb. 2728).

PLATE 128.—Fig. 1, a single head; Fig. 2, an involucral bract; Fig. 3, a single flower; Fig. 4, complete perianth segment and a limb showing position of the stamen; Fig. 5, stigma; Fig. 6, ovary.

F.P.S.A., 1924.

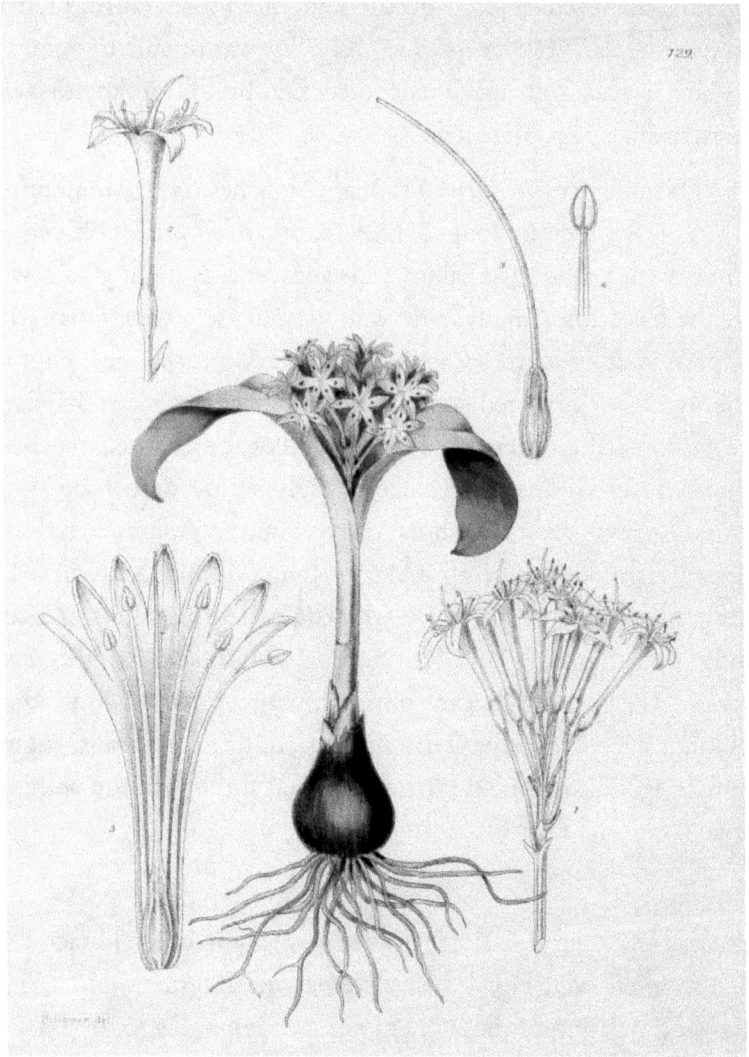

PLATE 129.

POLYXENA ENSIFOLIA.

Cape Province.

Liliaceae. *Tribe* Scilleae.

Polyxena, *Kunth*; *Benth. et Hook. f. Gen. Plant.*

Polyxena ensifolia, *SchÃ¶nland in Trans. Roy. Soc. S. Afr.*

On Plate 56 we figured a species of *Polyxena (P. haemanthoides),* and gave a few remarks on the genus. The present species, collected by Mr. A. J. Austin at Matjesfontein, C. P., was at first thought to be *P. pygmaea,* Kunth, but it differs in many respects from the published figures, and as it agrees quite well with SchÃ¶nlandâ€™s description of *P. ensifolia,* we have decided to place it under this species for the present. Dr. SchÃ¶nland, who saw the living plant at Pretoria, suggested that it was a species differing both from *P. ensifolia* and *P. pygmaea*; but until we know more about the genus both as regards the variability of the species and its distribution, it seems desirable to regard it as a form of P. ensifolia.

P. ensifolia is a pretty little plant. The leaves are semi-erect and the inflorescence of pale lilac flowers arises between them. It does quite well under cultivation, and has flowered for two seasons at the Division of Botany, Pretoria. We are indebted to Mr. Austin for the original bulbs.

Description:—Bulb 2Â·5 cm. long, 2Â·5 cm. in diameter, ovoid, covered with papery tunics. *Leaves* two, erect or spreading above, produced into a long clasping base 5-6 cm. long; the broadened lamina 5 cm. long, 3 cm. broad, ovate, obtuse, with reddish somewhat scarious margins, not distinctly veined, glabrous. *Inflorescence* corymbose, about 35-flowered. *Peduncle* 6 cm. long, subterete. *Bracts* 4Â·5 mm. long, ovate, acuminate, colourless. *Pedicels*, Â·35-1Â·6 cm. long, glabrous. *Perianth-tube* 1Â·5 cm. long, cylindric, gradually widening above; lobes 5Â·5 to 6 mm. long, 1Â·75 mm. broad, oblong, somewhat emarginate and hooded at the apex. *Stamens* in two rows; filaments 3 mm. long, terete, glabrous; anthers 1 mm. long, oblong. *Ovary* 3 mm. long, 1Â·5 mm. in diameter, ellipsoid; style 1Â·4 cm. long, terete; stigma minutely 3-lobed (National Herb. 2741).

PLATE 129.—Fig. 1, inflorescence; Fig. 2, a single flower; Fig. 3, flower laid open, showing position of stamens and pistil; Fig. 4, stamen; Fig. 5, pistil.

F.P.S.A., 1924.

PLATE 130.

HABENARIA FOLIOSA.

Cape Province, Orange Free State, Transvaal, Natal.

Orchidaceae. *Tribe* Ophrydeae.

Habenaria, *Willd.*; *Benth. et Hook. f. Gen. Plant.*
Habenaria foliosa, *Reichb. f. in Flora, 1865, 180; Fl.*

The species of *Habenaria* figured here has a wide range of distribution in South Africa. Starting from Swellendam in the south, it follows more or less the littoral strip as far as Port Alfred, and then spreads inland through the Transkei and East Griqualand into Natal, and through Basutoland and the eastern part of the Free State and up into the Transvaal Drakensbergen. The species is also met with in the Pretoria District, which is outside its normal range of distribution. In Basutoland the natives call it â€œ*Mametsana*,â€ meaning â€œthe mother of the small water.â€ The spur contains a watery substance which becomes jelly-like on exposure to air.

Around Pretoria the plant flowers in late summer, about February, after the rains, and is then frequently met with in the veld. The plate was prepared from specimens collected by Dr. I. B. Pole Evans, C.M.G., at Irene in February 1923.

Description:—*Plant* 30-40 cm. high. *Tuber* 5 cm. long, 2Â·5 cm. in diameter, ellipsoid, with thick cylindric roots arising from the junction of the stem and tuber. *Stem* covered with many amplexicaul leaves which pass gradually into the bracts. *Leaves* 4Â·5-8 cm. long, up to 3 cm. wide, ovate to ovate-lanceolate, stem-clasping at the base, obtuse or subapiculate at the apex, keeled with the midrib and 2 lateral veins prominent or distinct, glabrous. *Inflorescence* many-flowered, up to 13 cm. long. *Bracts* similar to the leaves but smaller. *Dorsal sepal* 1 cm. long, 9 mm. broad, ovate, deeply concave, faintly 3-nerved; lateral sepals 1Â·3 cm. long, 4Â·5 mm. broad, oblong, unequal sided, slightly cucullate at the apex, faintly 3-nerved. *Petals* 1Â·4-1Â·5 cm. long, 1 cm. broad, unequal sided, revolute on one margin near the apex, faintly 5-nerved. *Lip* 2 cm. long, with revolute margins and with two lateral filiform appendages at the base. *Spur* 3Â·5 cm. long, cylindric, clavate at the apex. *Rostellum* triangular in outline, the two side lobes notched. *Pollinia* sacs behind the rostellum. *Stigmas* separate, oblong, with small papillae at the junction of the stigma and pollinium sac. *Ovary* deeply grooved and angled (National Herb. 2730).

PLATE 130.—Fig. 1, median longitudinal section of flower; Fig. 2, front of flower, showing lip and column; Fig. 3, sepals; Fig. 4, a petal; Fig. 5, ovary; Fig. 6, pollinium.

F.P.S.A., 1924.

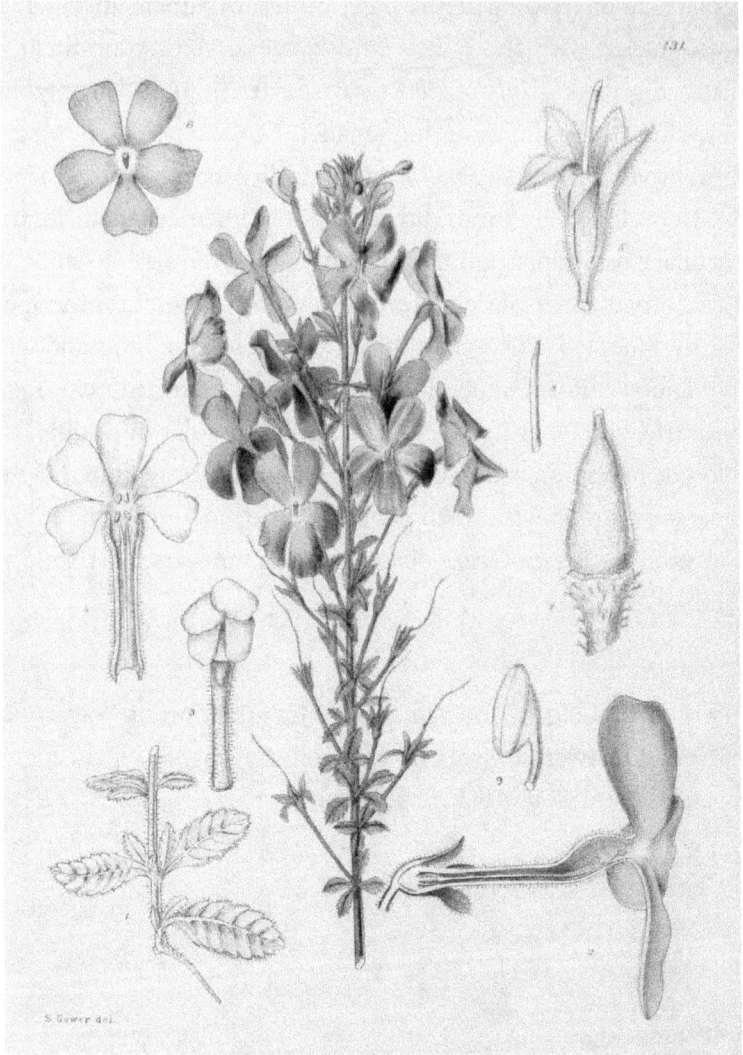

PLATE 131.

SUTERA GRANDIFLORA.
Transvaal.

Scrophulariaceae. *Tribe* Manuleae.

Sutera, *Roth.; Benth. et Hook. f. Gen. Plant.*
Sutera grandiflora, *Hiern.; Fl. Cap.*

Mr. E. E. Galpin, who collected this species round Barberton in 1889, described it in the *Kew Bulletin* (1895, p. 151) under the name of *Lyperia grandiflora.* The species is a native of the Barberton District of the Transvaal, but has not been extensively collected. Mr. Galpin describes it as â€œabundant amongst scrub on the hillsides and in the valleys around Barberton, flowering throughout the year, but chiefly in June and July.â€ In cultivation it grows to a rather dense bush 2 to 4 feet high, and flowers profusely. Very fine specimens are in cultivation at the National Botanic Gardens, Kirstenbosch, and we are indebted to the Director of the gardens for the fresh material from which the accompanying Plate was prepared. The species should prove a great acquisition to horticulturists.

Description:—An undershrub, viscid-pubescent erect, 0Â·4 to 1Â·2 m. high; branches alternate or opposite, ascending, leafy, rigid, rather robust, the lower elongated. *Leaves* mostly alternate, subfasciculate, oval-oblong, obtuse or subacute, more or less wedge-shaped at the base, crenate-serrate, hispid, scabrid, shortly petiolate, 0Â·6 to 3 cm. long, 3 to 8 mm. broad; lateral veins alternate, narrowly impressed on the upper face, hispid and raised on the lower. *Flowers* racemose, numerous, 2 to 3 cm. long; racemes terminal, simple, subcorymbose and rather dense at first, afterwards elongating and rather lax, deep purple, 4 to 30 cm. long; pedicels divaricate or ascending, glandular-pilose, moderately rigid, 1-flowered, alternate, 6 to 8 mm. long, the upper crowded; bracts basal, sublinear, solitary or subfasciculate. *Calyx* glandular-hispid, deeply 5-lobed, 6 to 8 mm. long; segments linear-oblong or spathulate or sublinear, obtuse. *Corolla-tube* shortly glandular-pubescent, 0Â·8 to 3 cm. long, subcylindrical, rather slender, slightly dilated and curved near the top; limb spreading, 2 to 3 cm. in diameter; lobes obovate-rotund, entire or retuse, 1 to 1Â·3 cm. long. *Stamens* included; style filiform, glabrous, about 1Â·5 cm. long; ovary sprinkled especially near the apex with small glands, otherwise glabrous. *Capsules* ovoid-oblong, minutely glandular, 1 cm. long; seeds very numerous, irregularly oblong, 0-5 mm. long. (*Flora Capensis*; National Herb. Pretoria, No. 2742.)

PLATE 131.—Fig. 1, portion of branch, showing leaves; Fig. 2, median longitudinal section of flower; Fig. 3, bud showing folding of petals; Fig. 4, corolla laid open; Fig. 5, calyx; Fig. 6, front view of petals; Fig. 7, ovary; Fig. 8, upper portion of style; Fig. 9, anther.

F.P.S.A., 1924.

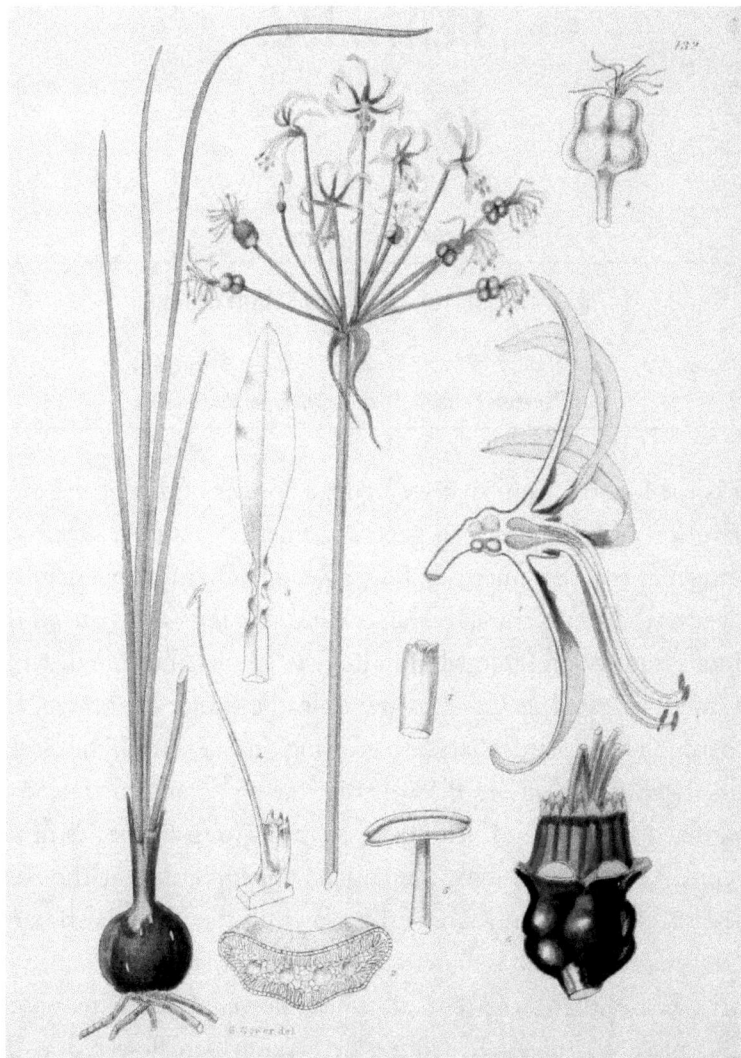

PLATE 132.

NERINE FRITHII.
Cape Province, Orange Free State.

AMARYLLIDACEAE. *Tribe* AMARYLLEAE.

NERINE, *Herb.*; *Benth. et Hook. f. Gen. Plant.*
Nerine Frithii, *L. Bolus in Ann. Bolus Herb.*

It is the first occasion that we figure a species of one of the most beautiful of South African genera, namely *Nerine. N. sarniensis*, known as the â€œGuernsey Lily,â€ and to mountaineers in the Cape as the â€œNerina,â€ ranks with *Disa uniflora* as one of the floral beauties of Table Mountain. The species illustrated, while it does not equal its Cape congener in the size of its flowers, is a charming little plant when seen growing. It differs from the closely allied genus *Hessea* (see Plate 43) in having dorsifixed instead of basifixed anthers, and belongs to a small group of species in the genus *Nerine* which have the anthers appendiculate at the base. The species has been successfully grown in the National Botanic Gardens at Kirstenbosch, near Cape Town, and was described by Mrs. L. Bolus from specimens which flowered at Kirstenbosch. Our plate was prepared from specimens which flowered at the Division of Botany, Pretoria. The plant figured differs from the description in not having two of the lobes of the staminal cup longer than the others, but Mrs. Bolus, who kindly examined our specimens, agrees that it is *N. Frithii*.

DESCRIPTION:—*Bulb* 2 cm. long, 1Â·7 cm. in diameter, ovoid-globose. *Leaves* present with the flowers, very often only two, up to 15 cm. long, 1 to 1Â·5 mm. broad, subfiliform, channelled above. *Inflorescence* an umbel of 5 to 7 flowers. *Peduncle* up to 20 cm. long, terete. *Spathe-valves* 2Â·5 to 3 cm. long, oblong, long-attenuate. *Pedicels* up to 3 cm. long. *Floral-bracts* 1 to 1Â·5 cm. long, thread-like, membranous. *Perianth-segments* spreading, at length recurved, 1.5 cm. long, 4 mm. broad, linear, acute, with undulate margins. *Stamens* declinate; filaments 0.35 to 6 mm. long, appendiculate at the base forming a cup 3 cm. long, somewhat lacerated above, with two lobes usually much exceeding the others; anthers 4 mm. long. *Ovary* obovate, with 2 ovules in each loculus. *Capsule* globose, 8 mm. in diameter. (National Herb. Pretoria, No. 2746.)

PLATE 132.—Fig. 1, median longitudinal section of flower; Fig. 2, cross section of leaf; Fig. 3, a single perianth-segment; Fig. 4, a stamen, showing position of appendage at the base; Fig. 5, anther; Fig. 6, fruit, showing cup formed of staminal appendages; Fig. 7, tip of style; Fig. 8, fruit.

F.P.S.A., 1924.

PLATE 133.

PROTEA ROUPPELLIAE.

Orange Free State, Transvaal, Swaziland, Cape Province, Natal.

PROTEACEAE. *Tribe* PROTEAE.

PROTEA, *Linn.*; *Benth. et Hook. f. Gen. Plant.*
Protea Rouppelliae, *Meisn. in DC. Prodr.*

This common and characteristic *Protea* of the Drakensbergen we figure here for the first time. It appears to have been originally collected by Burke and Zeyher on the Magaliesberg, and was described by Meisner and named after Mrs. Rouppell, who published an illustrated book of Cape flowers.

P. Rouppelliae forms extensive thickets on the slopes of the Drakensbergen, and in this respect resembles *P. mellifera, P. lepido-carpodendron* and *P. neriifolia* of the Cape Province. The species belongs to the same section of the genus as *P. compacta,* figured on Plate 84.

The specimens from which the accompanying Plate was painted were collected by Dr. I. B. Pole Evans, C.M.G., at the Devilâ€™s Kantoor in the Barberton District of the Transvaal.

DESCRIPTION:—A small tree 8 to 15 ft. high; branches villous or tomentose above, at length glabrescent. *Leaves* 10 to 15 cm. long, 2 to 4 cm. broad at the widest part, 4 mm. broad at the base, oblong-lanceolate or obovate-spathulate, acute, the younger densely villous or tomentose, at length glabrous, narrowed at the base, reticulately veined. *Head* shortly peduncled, 7 to 9 mm.

long, 5 to 10 cm. in diameter. *Involucral bracts* 10-seriate, silky-to-mentose, deep pink to pinky-white; outer ovate, obtuse, recurved to revolute, ciliate; inner with an obovate to obovate-oblong limb, gradually passing into the claw, shortly ciliate above, exceeding the flowers; perianth-sheath 4Â·5 cm. long, dilated and 3-keeled and 7-nerved below, loosely villous above the dilated portion; lip 3 cm. long, 3-awned, spreadingly villous; lateral awns 1Â·2 cm. long, linear, acuminate, purple, tomentose to villous; median awn 8 mm. long; fertile stamens 3; filaments 1 mm. long, flattened; anthers linear, 3 mm. long; apical glands 0Â·5 mm. long, oblong, acute; barren stamen acute, eglandular; ovary 4 mm. long, obovate in outline, densely covered with numerous long golden hairs; style 5 cm. long, curved, somewhat flattened, keeled below on the convex side, usually more or less shortly villous; stigma 4 mm. long, curved and kneed at the junction with the style. (*Flora Capensis*; National Herb. Pretoria, No. 2836.)

PLATE 133.—Fig. 1, receptacle; Fig. 2, inner bract; Fig. 3, single flower; Fig. 4, pistil.

F.P.S.A., 1924.

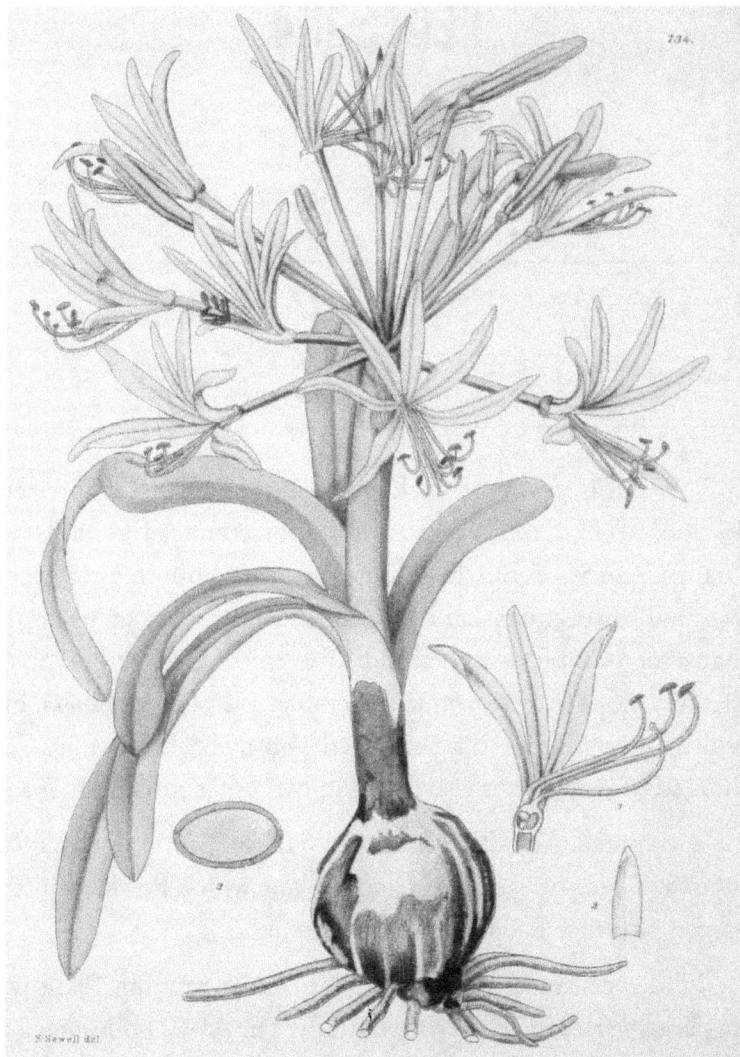

PLATE 134.

NERINE LUCIDA.
Cape Province, Orange Free State, Transvaal.

AMARYLLIDACEAE. *Tribe* AMARYLLEAE.

NERINE, Herb.; Benth. et Hook. f. Gen. Plant.
Nerine lucida, *Herb. Amaryllid. 283, t. 36, fig. 3; Fl.*

This species is, so far as we know, confined to the dry western portions of the Cape Province, S.W. Protectorate, Transvaal, and Orange Free State. Burchell found the plant both in Griqualand West and in Bechuanaland, and Burke on his journey up to the Transvaal found it near the Sand River in the Orange Free State. In habit the species very much resembles a dwarf *Brunsvigia*, but is distinguished from this genus by the obtusely angled ovary. The short stout peduncle is also found in two other species of *Nerine*.

A coloured plant of *N. lucida* was published in 1820 (*Botanical Register*, Plate 497), drawn from a plant which flowered in the garden of Prince Leopold of Saxe-Cobourg.

The specimens from which the accompanying Plate was prepared were collected at Vryburg by Mr. A. O. D. Mogg, and flowered at the Division of Botany, Pretoria, in 1924.

DESCRIPTION:—*Bulb* globose, 4 cm. in diameter, produced into a neck about 4 cm. long. *Leaves* 6, contemporary with the flowers, about 18 cm. long, about 12 mm. broad, strap-shaped, obtuse, bright green. *Peduncle* lateral, about 12 cm. long, compressed. *Inflorescence* an umbel of 20 flowers. *Pedicels* up to 7 cm. long, shortly hairy. *Spathe-valves* ovate-lanceolate, membranous, shorter than the pedicels. *Perianth-segments* 15 mm. long, 5 mm. broad, lanceolate-linear, obtuse. *Stamens* declinate, almost as long as the perianth segments. *Ovary* obtusely trigonous; style declinate, as long as the stamens. (National Herb., Pretoria, No. 2835.)

PLATE 134.—Fig. 1, median longitudinal section of a flower; Fig. 2, upper portion of perianth lobe, showing apex; Fig. 3, cross-section through the peduncle.

F.P.S.A., 1924.

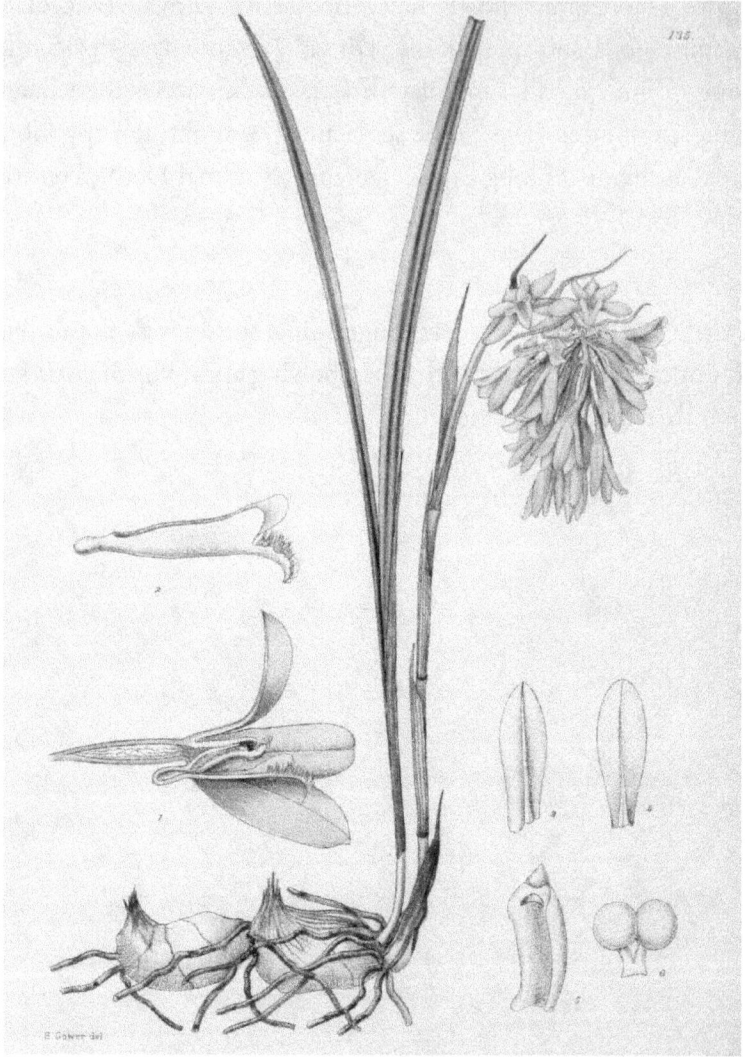

PLATE 135.

EULOPHIA LEONTOGLOSSA.

Orange Free State, Transvaal, Cape Province, Natal.

ORCHIDACEAE. *Tribe* VANDEAE.

EULOPHIA, *R.Br.*; *Benth. et Hook. f. Gen. Plant.*

Eulophia leontoglossa, *Reichb. f. in Flora, 1881, 329; Fl.*

This charming little *Eulophia* is found in the summer months round Pretoria growing in the grass veld, and is fairly abundant. Like many other plants found in the neighbourhood of the Magaliesberg, it was collected by the travellers Burke and Zeyher. It ranges from the Maclear Division, through the Orange Free State, to Natal and the Transvaal.

E. leontoglossa belongs to the same small group (four species) in the genus as *E. Zeyheri* (figured on Plate 119), which is characterised by the flowers being arranged in congested racemes or short heads. Like *E. Zeyheri* also, the tubers are arranged in a linear series and resemble large oval beads.

Our figure was made from specimens collected by Dr. I. B. Pole Evans, C.M.G., at Irene, near Pretoria.

DESCRIPTION:—*Tubers* subglobose, about 2 cm. broad; leaves 2 or 3 in a fascicle, linear or lanceolate-linear, acute or acuminate, 10 to 36 cm. long, 1Â·25 to 8 mm. broad. *Scapes* erect, 10 to 35 cm. long, with a few lanceolate acuminate sheaths below. *Flowerheads* congested or rarely oblong, 2Â·5 to 5 cm. long; bracts linear or linear-lanceolate, acuminate, 1Â·3 to 2 cm. long; pedicels 6 to

8 mm. long; lip 3-lobed, elliptic-oblong, narrowed at the base, about as long as the petals; side-lobes somewhat divergent, oblong, obtuse or truncate, short; front lobe elliptic-oblong, obtuse; disc with 5 obscure keels below, papillose above, and with the surface of the front lobe strongly papillose all over; spur oblong or subclavate, obtuse, 4 mm. long; column clavate, 4 mm. long. (*Fl. Cap.*)

PLATE 135.—Fig. 1, median longitudinal section of flower; Fig. 2, lip; Fig. 3, sepal; Fig. 4, petal; Fig. 5, column; Fig. 6, pollinia.

F.P.S.A., 1924.

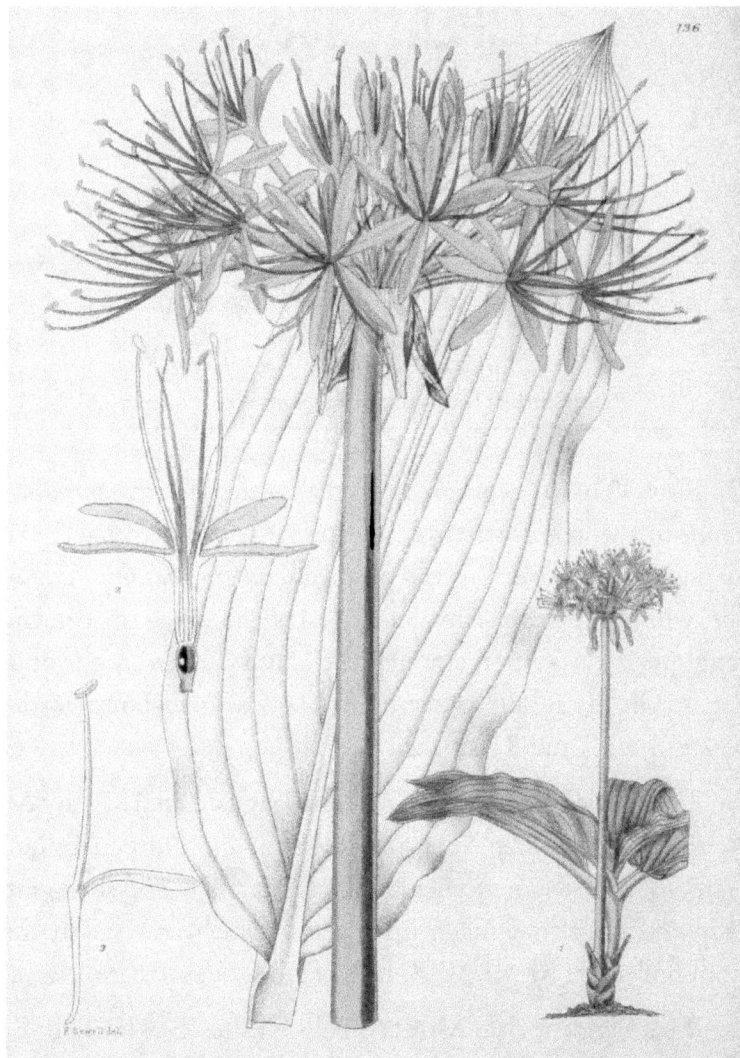

PLATE 136.

HAEMANTHUS Katharinae.
Natal, Transvaal.

AMARYLLIDACEAE. TRIBE AMARYLLEAE.

Haemanthus, Linn.; Benth. et Hook. f. Gen. Plant.
Haemanthus Katharinae, *Baker in Gard. Chron. 1877.*

On Plate 32 of this work we figured a species of *Haemanthus* (*H. natalensis*) which differs from the present species in having the involucral-bracts erect instead of spreading. *Haemanthus Katharinae*, with its spreading involucral-bracts and perianth-segments, is unique in this respect amongst the South African species of the genus. On the inflorescence figured was an odd flower with 8 perianth-lobes and 8 stamens.

The species was introduced into England in 1877 by Mr. Keith, who was then Superintendent of the Durban Botanic Gardens. In 1884 an excellent figure (Plate 6778) appeared in the *Botanical Magazine*, made from plants which flowered at Kew from bulbs sent by Mr. W. B. Lyle of Kirkly Vale Estate, Natal.

We are indebted to Mr. P. S. Follwell, Isezela, Natal, for our specimen, which was cultivated at the Division and flowered in January 1923.

DESCRIPTION:—*Stem* up to 18 cm. long. *Leaves* 5 to 6 to a plant, contemporary with the flowers, 20 to 30 cm. long, 10 to 13 cm. broad, oblong, shortly mucronate; petiole 3 to 4 cm. long, channelled above. *Peduncle* lateral, terete, up to 40 cm. long. *Inflo-*

rescence a many-flowered umbel. *Bracts* 6, membranous, spreading or reflexed. *Pedicels* slender, 2Â·5 to 4 cm. long. *Perianth-tube* 2 cm. long; lobes 2Â·5 cm. long, linear-lanceolate, spreading or reflexed. *Stamens* inserted at the throat of the perianth-tube; filaments 4Â·5 cm. long, erect; anthers 3 mm. long. *Ovary* ellipsoid; style up to 6 cm. long; stigma simple. (National Herb. Pretoria, No. 2837.)

PLATE 136.—Fig. 1, plant much reduced; Fig. 2, median longitudinal section of the flower; Fig. 3, perianth segment showing attachment of stamen.

F.P.S.A., 1924.

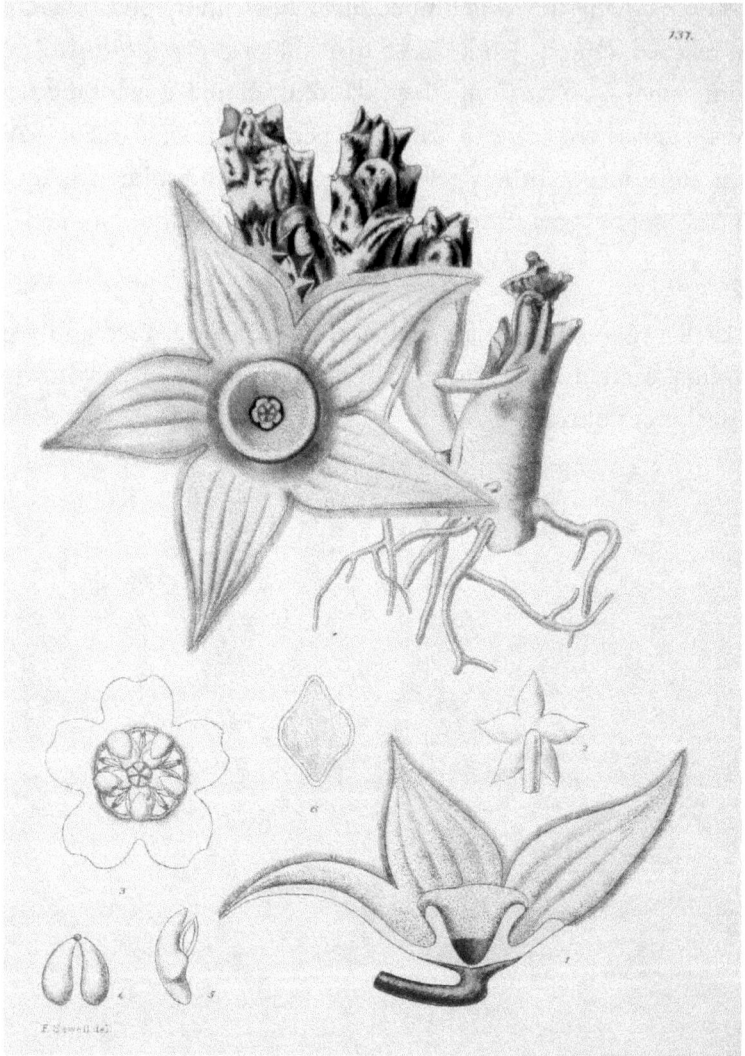

PLATE 137.

DIPLOCYATHA CILIATA.

Cape Province.

ASCLEPIADACEAE. Tribe STAPELIEAE.

DIPLOCYATHA, N. E. Br. in Journ. Linn. Soc.

Diplocyatha ciliata, *N. E. Br. l.c.; Fl.*

When Mr. Brown first described this remarkable genus in 1880, he only knew of Massonâ€™s and Thunbergâ€™s specimens, and up to the time of the account in the *Flora Capensis* (1909) Dr. Marloth was the only recent collector who had found the plant. Mrs. D. van der Bijl, of Abrahamâ€™s Kraal, in the Beaufort West District, who has contributed several interesting plants we have figured, sent us specimens in 1919, which flowered at the Division of Botany, Pretoria, this year.

It was figured in a coloured plate by Masson in 1796, and our present Plate is the first to be produced since then. A pencil drawing of a portion of the flower, the corona and the pollinia, accompanied Brownâ€™s original description, and while our specimen differs in some minor points from the drawings, we have no hesitation in referring it to the same species. The flower is rather handsome, and devoid of the objectionable smell usually associated with the members of the tribe *Stapelieae*.

DESCRIPTION:—*Stems* decumbent and ascending, 4 to 6Â·5 cm. long, 1Â·5 to 2 cm. thick excluding the teeth, obtusely 4-angled, with stout conical acute teeth 4 to 6 mm. long, glabrous,

green, mottled with purple. *Flowers* subsolitary from near the base
or middle of the stems; pedicels 1 to 2 cm. long, erect, glabrous.
Sepals about 6 mm. long, ovate or ovate-lanceolate, acute, glabrous.
Corolla about 7Â·5 cm. in diameter, smooth and glabrous outside,
densely papillate-rugose on the inner face, according to Thunberg
and Masson, greyish, with the tips of the papillae reddish, but
according to Massonâ€™s figure, pale yellowish with a greyish ring
around the mouth of the tube, minutely dotted with red; tube
campanulate, apparently slightly raised at its mouth around the
very thick recurved papillate-rugose rim of the inner tube, which
is densely covered with stiff purple hairs at the base around and
under the corona; lobes about 2Â·5 cm. long, 1Â·5 to 2 cm. broad,
spreading, ovate, acute, ciliate from base to apex with clavate
vibratile white hairs; outer corona-lobes arising above the base of
the staminal column, connate at the base, somewhat spreading,
with the free 2/3 to 1Â·5 mm. long, 2 mm. broad, transverse or
subquadrate, very obtusely or subacutely bifid, glabrous, apparently yellowish dotted with purple-brown; inner corona-lobes
incumbent on the backs of the anthers, about 1Â·5 mm. long,
thick, ovate, acute, or acuminate with the tips produced into a
very short erect point, apparently yellowish, dotted and marked
with purple-brown. (*Flora Capensis*; National Herb. Pretoria, No.
2841.)

PLATE 137.—Fig. 1, median longitudinal section of the flower
with corona removed; Fig. 2, sepals; Fig. 3, corona; Fig. 4, pollinia;
Fig. 5, inner corona lobe showing pollen-sac; Fig. 6, cross-section
of stem.

F.P.S.A., 1924.

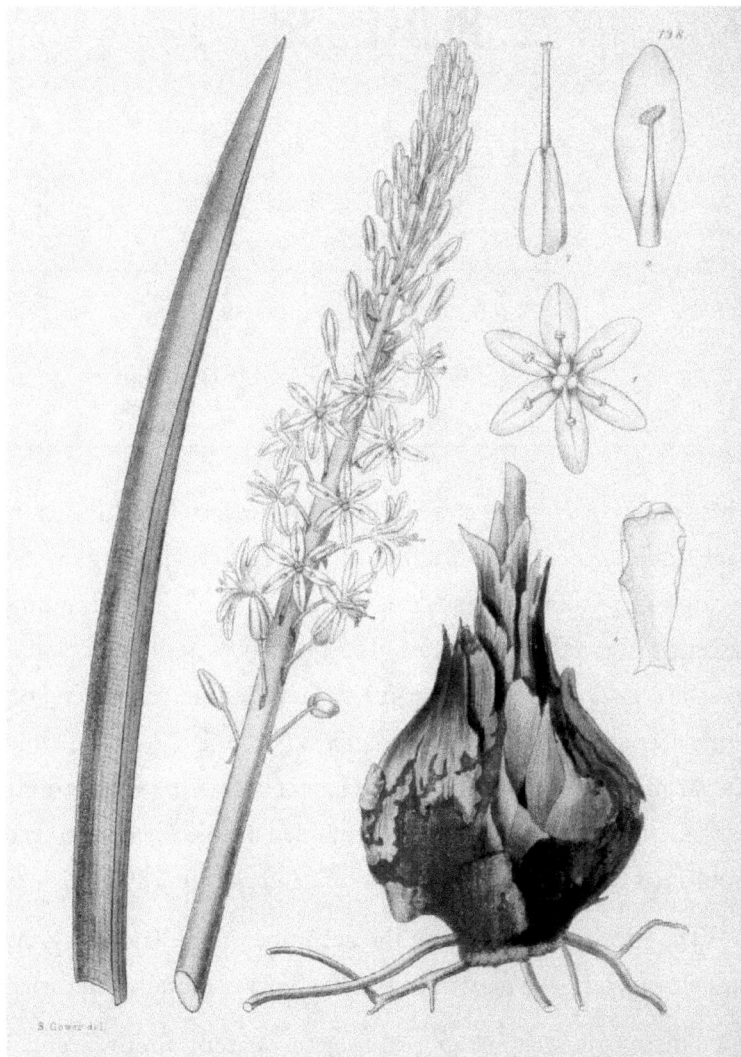

PLATE 138.

URGINEA BURKEI.

Transvaal, Cape Province.

Liliaceae. *Tribe* Scilleae.

Urginea, *Steinh.*; *Benth. et Hook. f. Gen. Plant.*

Urginea Burkei, *Baker; Fl.*

This species of *Urginea* is well known to the farmers of the Transvaal under the common name of â€œTransvaal Slangkop,â€ owing to the somewhat striking resemblance of the young inflorescence to a snakeâ€™s head. The plant is extremely poisonous to stock, and in early spring many fatalities are reported. For a fuller account of this plant see Bulletin No. 7, 1922, of the Union Department of Agriculture. Burke first collected the species on the Magaliesberg about 1830, but it remained undescribed until Baker published his description in the *Flora Capensis* in 1896.

The specimen figured on the accompanying Plate was grown and flowered in the garden of the Division of Botany, Pretoria.

Description:—*Bulb* globose, tunicated, about 7 cm. in diameter. *Leaves* about 26 cm. long, about 1 cm. broad, linear. *Peduncle* 17 cm. long, terete. *Inflorescence* a cylindric raceme, 17 cm. long. *Pedicels* ascending; the lower 1 cm. long. *Bracts* small, oblong, subacuminate, membranous, spurred at the base, deciduous. *Perianth* 1 cm. long; segments oblong-lanceolate, white with a brown keel. *Stamens* shorter than the perianth-segments.

Ovary 4 mm. long, obtusely trigonous; style 3Â·5 mm. long. (National Herb. Pretoria, No. 2647.)

PLATE 138.—Fig. 1, surface view of flower; Fig. 2, perianth-segment with stamen; Fig. 3, pistil; Fig. 4, bract.

F.P.S.A., 1924.

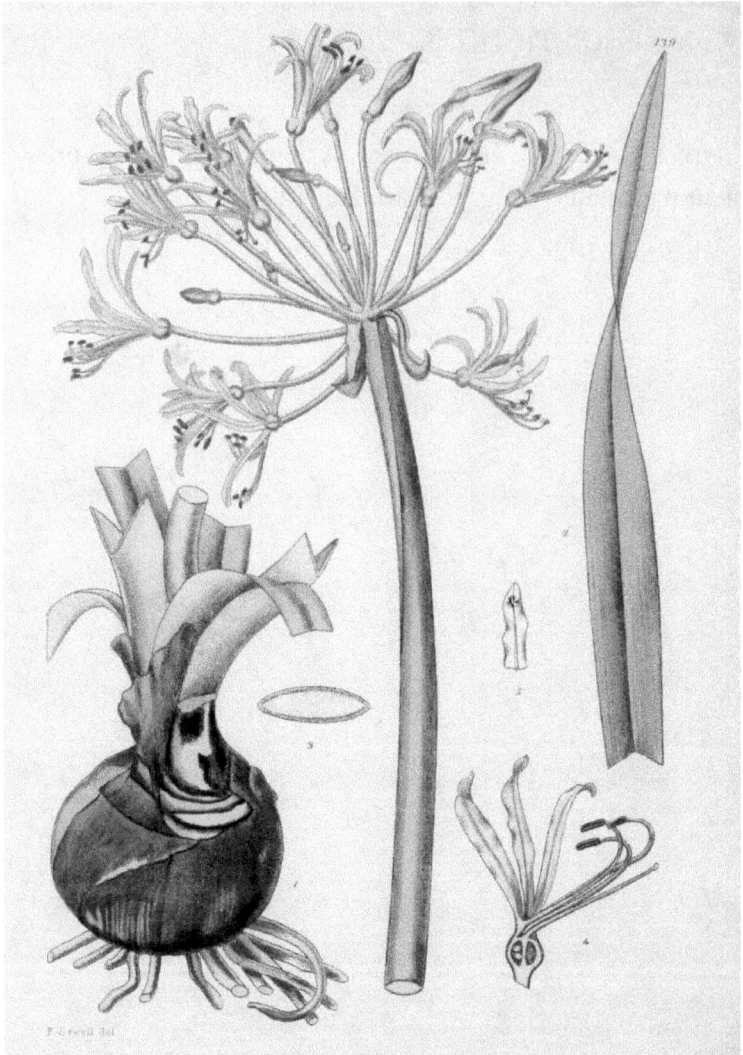

PLATE 139.

NERINE FLEXUOSA
var. SANDERSONI.
Transvaal.

AMARYLLIDACEAE. TRIBE AMARYLLEAE.

NERINE, *Herb.*; *Benth. et Hook. f. Gen. Plant.*
Nerine flexuosa, *Herb. App. 19*; *Fl.*

Our Plate represents a variety of *Nerine flexuosa* found in the Transvaal, which is distinguished from the type in having a more robust inflorescence. It very much resembles *N. lucida*, figured on Plate 134, but the peduncle is much longer and not so stout. Very little is known about this variety. It is recorded in the *Flora Capensis* as collected by Sanderson in the Transvaal, and does not appear to have been found again by any recent collector. When planted in a mass it makes a very effective display as soon as the flowers appear.

The plants from which this Plate was prepared were grown at the Division of Botany, Pretoria, but no information is available as to where the bulbs originally came from.

DESCRIPTION:—*Bulb* globose, 7 cm. in diameter. *Leaves* about 7, 30 cm. long, 2Â·7 cm. broad, strap-shaped, usually twisted. *Umbel* about 25-flowered. *Peduncle* up to 40 cm. long, elliptic in cross-section. *Pedicels* up to 7 cm. long, slender. *Spathe-valves* 4 cm. long, ovate, acuminate. *Perianth-segments* about 4 cm. long, crisped in the upper half. *Stamens* declinate; filaments almost as long as the perianth-segments. *Ovary* globose, obtusely 3-angled; style declinate, as long as the filaments; stigma simple.

PLATE 139.—Fig. 1, bulb; Fig. 2, leaf; Fig. 3, cross-section of peduncle; Fig. 4, median longitudinal section of a flower; Fig. 5, upper portion of perianth-segment, showing tuft of papillose hairs.

F.P.S.A., 1924.

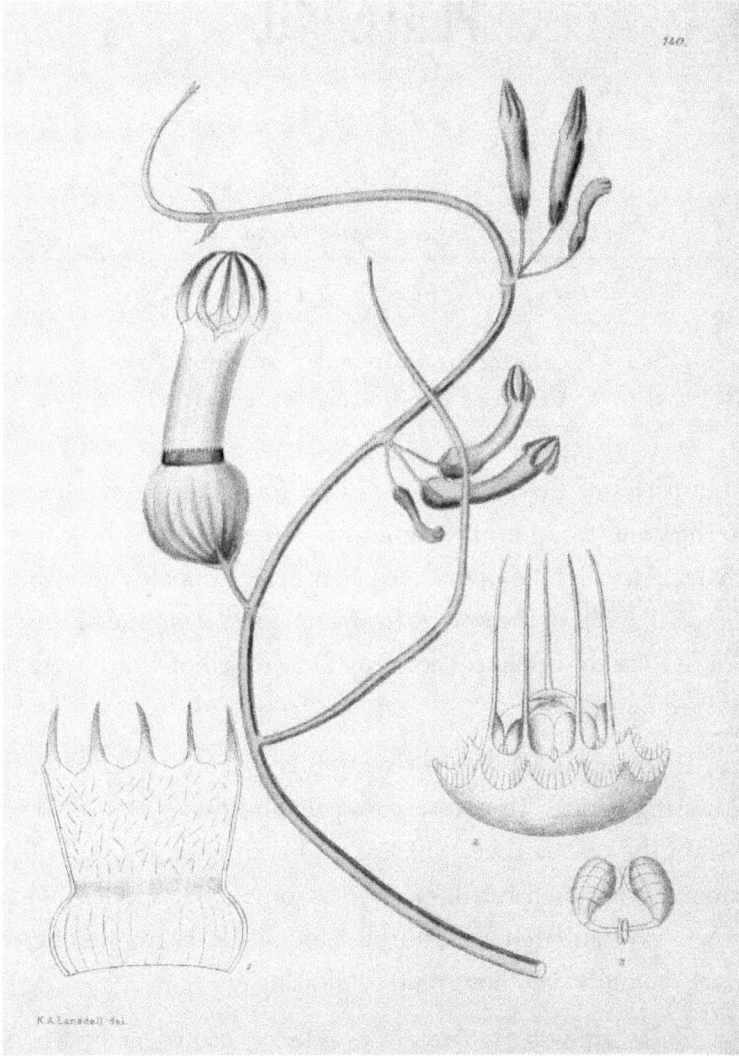

PLATE 140.

Asclepiadaceae. Tribe Ceropegieae.

Ceropegia, Linn.; Benth. et Hook. f. Gen. Plant.

Ceropegia ampliata, *E. Mey. Comm. 194; Fl.*

The species of *Ceropegia*, figured here for the first time, belongs to the same group in the genus as *C. Meyeri* (Plate 30), which is characterised by the tips of the petals being connate and forming a cage-like top to the flower. *Ceropegia ampliata* is one of the five South African species collected by DrÂ¨ge, all of which were described by E. Meyer.

The plant is a twiner or scrambler, devoid of leaves at the flowering period. The flowers are pale green with a purple band within the corolla-tube, which is visible through the wall of the tube. It is not such a striking plant as some of the species we have previously figured, but the purple band on a background of green gives the individual flower a very pleasing effect.

Our Plate was prepared from a living plant lent by Mr. W. Haygarth to the late Dr. J. Medley Wood.

Description:—*Stem* succulent, twining or scrambling, leafless at the time of flowering, glabrous. *Leaves* only seen at the young tips of the stems, soon deciduous, minute, 2 to 2Â·5 mm. long, lanceolate, acute, glabrous. *Flowers* 2 to 4 together at the nodes, successively developed; pedicels 0Â·6 to 1Â·3 cm. long, glabrous. *Sepals* 2 to 3 mm. long, lanceolate, acuminate, glabrous. *Corolla-tube* in dried specimens 2Â·5 to 5 cm. long, 0Â·8 to 1Â·2 cm. in diameter, cylindric and slightly or not at all inflated at the base, but on the living plant, according to a drawing, 5 cm. long, globosely and somewhat lobulate-inflated and about 2Â·5 cm. in diameter at the base, cylindric and 1Â·3 cm. in diameter above, not dilated at the apex, pale green, with a narrow purple transverse band at the top of the inflation inside, glabrous outside, covered inside with long simple hairs, longer and more matted at the purple band and above than in the lower part; lobes 0Â·8 to 1Â·2 cm. long, 5 to 6 mm. broad at the base, lanceolate from a deltoid base, acute, erectly connivent and connate at the tips, replicate or with reflexed margins, glabrous on both sides and not ciliate, green, spotted with darker green, becoming olive-brown when dried, probably with a velvety sheen on the inner surface; outer corona cup-shaped, equally 10-toothed; teeth about 1 mm. long, narrowly deltoid, acute, hairy on the inner surface; inner corona-lobes 4 to 5 mm. long, very slenderly filiform, connivent-erect, dorsally-connected by vertical plates to the outer corona at the base. (*Flora Capensis.*)

PLATE 140.—Fig. 1, corolla laid open; Fig. 2, outer and inner corona, showing the pollinia; Fig. 3, pollinia.

F.P.S.A., 1924.

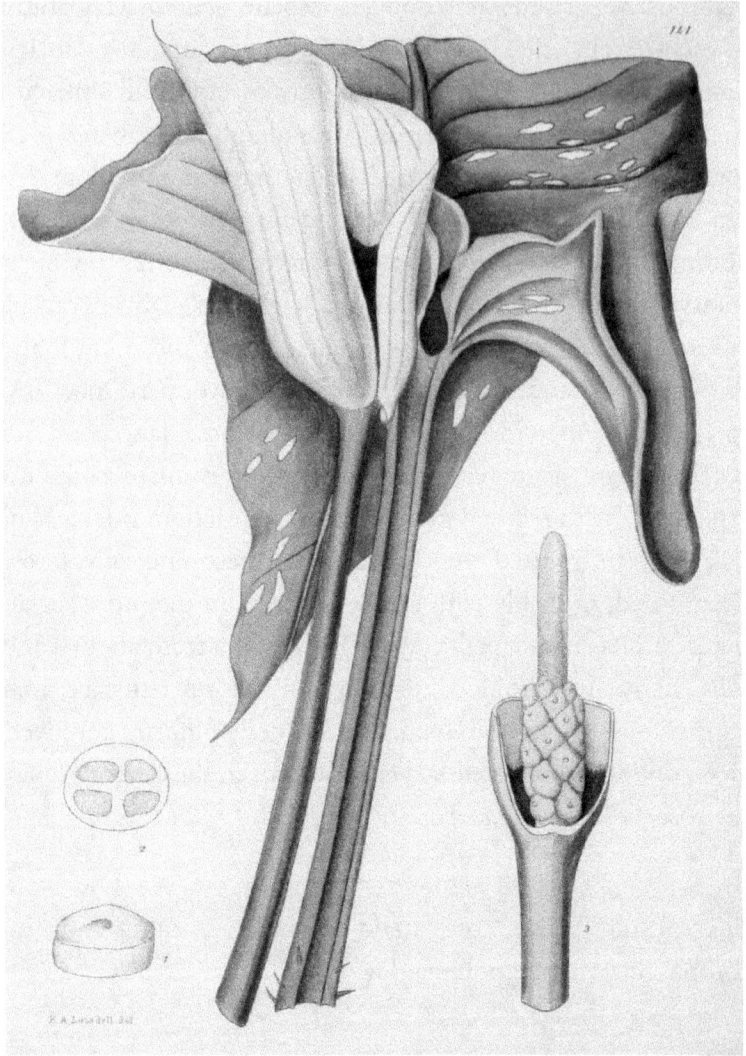

PLATE 141.

AROIDEAE. *Tribe* PHILODENDREAE.

RICHARDIA, *Kunth*; *Benth. et Hook. f. Gen. Plant.*
Richardia melanoleuca, *Hook. f. in Bot. Mag. t. 5765; Fl.*

ON Plate 10 we figured a species of *Richardia* (*R. angustifolia*) found in the Transvaal and Basutoland, and on comparing that plate with the present one, illustrating a Natal species, the most striking difference noticed is the different colour of the spathes. In both species the spathes are blotched at the base, but the leaves of *R. melanoleuca* are usually covered with translucent spots due to the loss of chlorophyll (for further details see Saxton in *Trans. Roy. Soc. S. Afr.* vol. iii. p. 136).

The species is fairly common in parts of Natal, and is often found cultivated in local gardens. It was introduced into England and flowered there in 1868.

Our plate was prepared from specimens collected at Krantz Kloof, near Durban.

DESCRIPTION:—Root tuberous. *Petiole* of leaf 15 to 35 cm. long, furrowed on the inner surface, with soft bristles on the lower parts; blade 10 to 25 cm. long, 12 to 20 cm. broad across the basal lobes, cordate, deltoid or ovate-deltoid, acute, with a subulate point, hastate or sagittate at the base, green, shining, glabrous, covered with numerous translucent spots. *Spathe* 5 to

8 cm. long, obliquely subtruncate at the mouth; spadix shortly stipitate, cylindric. *Ovary* sessile; stigma sessile or subsessile. *Anthers* numerous. *Staminodes* none.

PLATE 141.—Fig. 1, ovary; Fig. 2, cross-section through fruit; Fig. 3, spadix with spathe removed.

F.P.S.A., 1924.

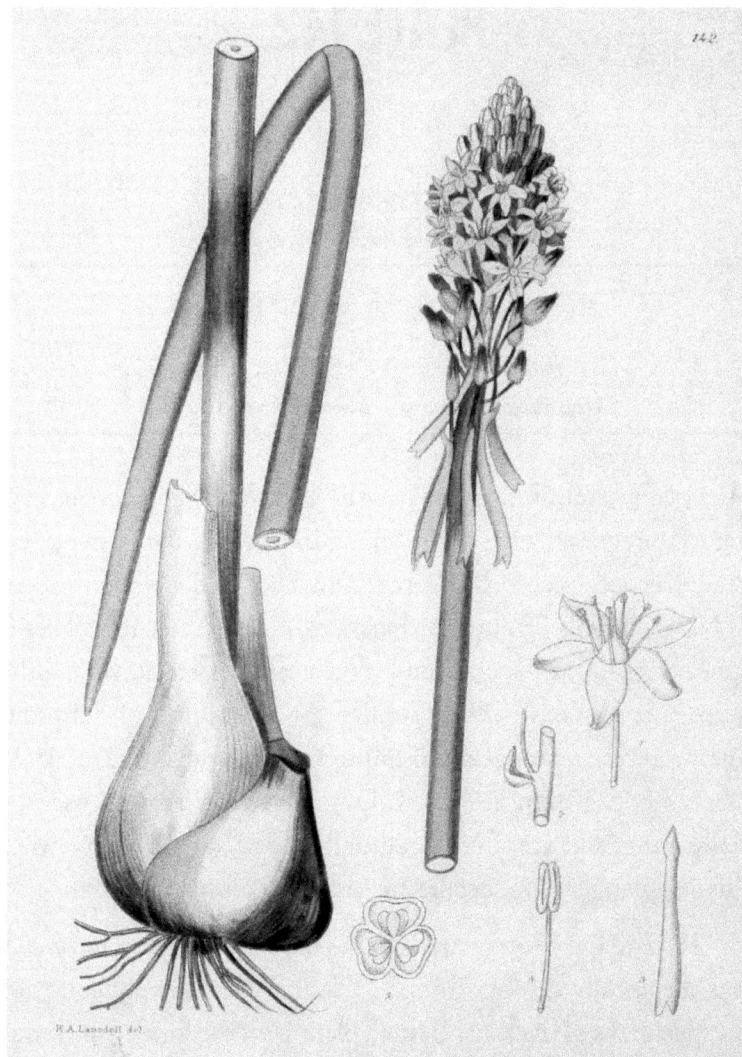

PLATE 142.

URGINEA MACROCENTRA.
Cape Province, Natal.

LILIACEAE. *Tribe* SCILLEAE.

URGINEA, *Steinh.; Benth. et Hook. f. Gen. Plant.*
Urginea macrocentra, *Baker in Gard. Chron. 1887.*

THIS plant, commonly known as the â€œNatal Slangkop,â€ owing to the resemblance of the young inflorescence to a snakeâ€™s
head, has been recorded from the Umvoti District along the coast
of Natal, and also from the Transkei. The inflorescence makes its
appearance in early spring, and is then eaten by stock, when other
herbage is scarce, with fatal results (for an account of symptoms
due to â€œslangkopâ€ poisoning see Bulletin No. 7 of 1922,
Dept. Agric. Union S. Africa). During the spring months, especially if the rains are later than usual, losses of stock in parts where
this â€œslangkopâ€ occurs are of almost annual occurrence.

The late Dr. Wood stated that he did not think *U. macrocentra*
was specifically distinct from *U. lilacina.* He carefully compared
his specimens of the latter-named plant with the former, and could
detect no difference, and suggested that the specimens described
by Baker as *U. lilacina* were merely *U. macrocentra* which had lost
the conspicuous spurs, these being very early deciduous.

Our plate was prepared from specimens collected near
Merebank outside Durban, and cultivated at the Natal Herbarium.

DESCRIPTION:—*Bulb* large, globose, 4 to 6 cm. in diameter.

Leaf single, 30 to 60 cm. long, 1 mm. in diameter, terete, purple-red at the base. *Peduncle* 70 to 90 cm. long, 7 mm. in diameter, terete. *Inflorescence* a dense cylindric raceme 8 to 15 cm. long and 2 to 3 cm. in diameter. *Bracts* with a long reflexed spur; spur 2 to 3 cm. long, 4 mm. broad at the base, convolute, bifid. *Perianth-segments* 6 mm. long, oblong-lanceolate. *Stamens* shorter than the perianth-segments. *Ovary* sessile; style short.

PLATE 142.—Fig. 1, single flower; Fig. 2, part of inflorescence axis showing pedicel and bract with the spur removed; Fig. 3, spur; Fig. 4, stamen; Fig. 5, cross-section of ovary.

F.P.S.A., 1924.

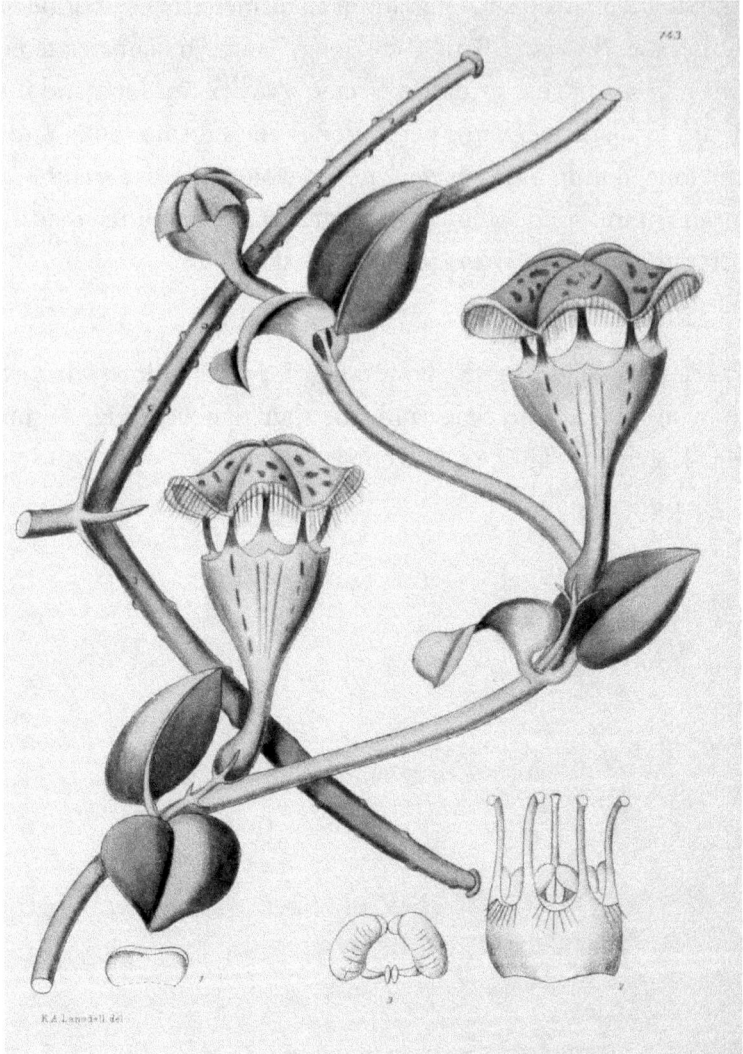

PLATE 143.

CEROPEGIA SANDERSONI.

Natal, Zululand.

Asclepiadaceae. Tribe Ceropegieae.

Ceropegia, Linn.; Benth. et Hook. f. Gen. Plant.
Ceropegia Sandersoni, *Decne ex Hook. f. in Bot. Mag. t. 5792; Fl.*

On Plate 39 we figured a species of *Ceropegia (C. Rendalii)*, which is one of a group of four species characterised by the corolla-lobes being united into an umbrella-like canopy supported by 5 short stalks. The species on the accompanying plate is another of this group, and should be compared with *C. Rendalii* and *C. tristis* (Plate 44).

The original description and plate appeared in the *Botanical Magazine* in 1869, and were based on specimens sent to Kew by Mr. Sanderson in 1868, and which subsequently flowered there. The plant lends itself very well to cultivation in the green-house, and is an object of beauty and curiosity when in flower. It does not appear to have been extensively collected, and may not be very common. In its native habitat it flowers during the month of February.

As far as we are aware, there is no local name for the plant, and we would therefore suggest â€œSandersonâ€™s Canopy Flowerâ€ as an appropriate name. According to Gerrard the stems and leaves are eaten by the Kaffirs and have an agreeable, sauce-like flavour.

Our plate was prepared from living specimens collected by Mr. W. J. Haygarth at Entumeni, Zululand.

DESCRIPTION:—â€œRoots tuberous similar to those of a Dahliaâ€⊠ (Gerrard); stem twining, 3 to 4 mm. thick, fleshy, glabrous, slightly rough to the touch; leaves fleshy, glabrous; petiole 2 to 6 mm. long, stout; blade 1Â·5 to 4Â·5 cm. long, 1Â·5 to 2Â·5 cm. broad, ovate-lanceolate to broadly cordate-ovate, acute or shortly cuspidate-acute, light green; cymes with 2 to 4 flowers, developed singly, glabrous; peduncles 4 to 10 mm. long, 3 to 4 mm. thick; pedicels 6 to 10 mm. long, nearly or quite 3 mm. thick, becoming stouter in fruit; sepals 6 to 7 mm. long, 2 mm. broad, narrowly oblong, acute, longitudinally folded, glabrous; corolla-tube curved, 3 to 4 mm. long, with an oblong inflation 6 mm. in diameter at the base, narrowed above and enlarged to 1Â·5 cm. or 2 cm. in diameter at the funnel-shaped mouth, glabrous with the exception of a few hairs at the very base inside; striped with green and white on the upper part outside and within, light green on the inflation outside, dull greyish-or purplish-green within, with numerous ribs, which abruptly terminate at the base of the purple contracted part; lobes united into a flattish 5-keeled umbrella-like canopy 3 to 4 cm. in diameter, supported on 5 short claws, with 5 broad obtuse slightly bifid marginal much-arched lobes, ciliate with vibratile white hairs, its centre distinctly depressed, with a 6-pointed tubercle above and a 5-ribbed projection beneath, yellowish-green, spotted with light green above and with brighter green underneath, with the ribbed projection beneath and some spots around it blackish-purple; outer corona 1 mm. long, cup-shaped, not pentagonal, truncate, entire, whitish, with the margin and at its junction with the inner corona-lobes purple-brown, ciliate with white hairs; inner corona-lobes 3 mm. long, incumbent on the backs of the anthers, with erect filiform tips, recurved at the apex, dorsally connected to the outer corona at the base, glabrous, white; follicles horizontally diverging, 7 to 14 cm. long, 6Â·5 to 7 mm. thick, terete, tapering from about the middle to a slightly dilated umbonate apex about 4 mm. in diameter, irregularly rugose and tuberculate, glabrous, green, stained with dull purplish. (*Flora Capensis.*)

PLATE 143.—Fig. 1, outer corona lobe; Fig. 2, inner corona lobes; Fig. 3, pollinia.

F.P.S.A., 1924.

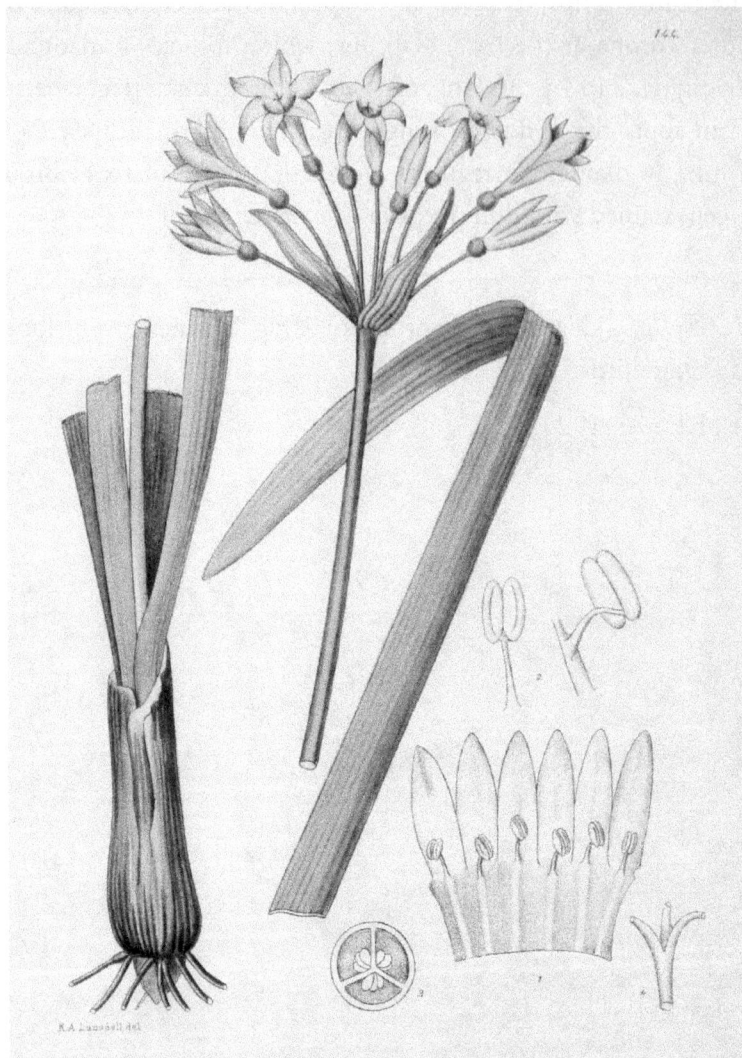

PLATE 144.

ANOIGANTHUS BREVIFLORUS.
Cape Province, Natal, Swaziland.

AMARYLLIDACEAE. TRIBE AMARYLLEAE.

ANOIGANTHUS, Baker; Benth. et Hook. f. Gen. Plant.
Anoiganthus breviflorus, *Baker in Journ. Bot. 1878, p. 76; Fl.*

IN 1889 a good coloured plate of this plant was reproduced in the *Botanical Magazine*. The plate was prepared from plants sent to Kew by the late Dr. Medley Wood, and which flowered freely there in the open. *Anoiganthus breviflorus* is readily distinguished from species of *Cyrtanthus* (species of which we figured in earlier plates) by having basifixed, not versatile anthers. It is a fairly widely distributed species, being found as far south as Somerset East, and spreading northward through the eastern parts of the Cape Province into Natal, Zululand, Basutoland, Swaziland and to Broken Hill, N.W. Rhodesia. The same yellow colour of the flowers is found in species of *Cyrtanthus*, but specimens with white flowers have been recorded.

The species does quite well in cultivation, and in its native habitat thrives in swampy and marshy ground.

Our plate was prepared from plants collected near Springfield (Durban), Natal.

[There appears to be a second and quite distinct species (*A. luteus* Baker) of this interesting little genus, though Baker in the *Flora Capensis* treated it as a variety. That it is distinct enough to be regarded as a species was very strongly supported by the late Dr. J. Medley Wood. According to him *A. breviflorus* grows in swampy ground, commencing at about 1500 ft. above sea level, and is found upwards to 4000 ft. He observed it occasionally to 4 ft. in height, but the average was 2 to 3 ft. On the other hand, *A. luteus* appears on grassy hills and plains from just above sea level to 2000 ft., but never in swamps. During the flowering stage it is rarely more than about 1 ft. high, but afterwards, in fruit, the scape lengthens considerably and often attains 2 ft. in length. These observations by Dr. Wood are confirmed by a critical examination of the specimens at Kew. The flowers and leaves appear to be always contemporaneous in *A. breviflorus*, but in *A. luteus* the flowers appear first and the leaves are very small. Further notes by Natal botanists would be welcome.—J. H.]

DESCRIPTION:—*Bulb* ovoid, white, 2 to 3 cm. in diameter, with a short neck and brown membranous tunics. *Leaves* 3 to 4, contemporary with the flowers, 4 to 30 cm. long, 7 to 14 mm. broad, strap-shaped, obtuse, strongly-nerved, glabrous. *Peduncle* 8 to 20 cm. long, about 4 mm. in diameter, slender, erect. *Spathe-valves* 4 to 5 cm. long, 4 mm. broad at the base lanceolate. *Pedicels* 2 to 4 cm. long, erect. *Inflorescence* a 2-to 10-flowered umbel. *Perianth-tube* 5 mm. long; lobes 15 mm. long, lanceolate, acute. *Stamens* included, in 2 series; anthers basifixed. *Ovary* glabrous; style slender; stigmas 3, overtopping the stamens.

PLATE 144.—Fig. 1, perianth laid open; Fig. 2, stamens; Fig. 3, cross-section of ovary; Fig. 4, style-branches.

F.P.S.A., 1924.

PLATE 145.

BURCHELLIA BUBALINA.
Cape Province, Natal, Transvaal.

RUBIACEAE. *Tribe* GARDENIEAE.

BURCHELLIA, *R. Br.; Benth. et Hook. f. Gen. Plant.*
Burchellia bubalina, *Sims Bot. Mag. t. 2339 (1822).*
Lonicera bubalina, Linn. f. Suppl. 146 (1781). Burchellia
capensis, R. Br. in Ker. Bot. Reg. t. 466 (1820); Fl.

Burchellia bubalina is known locally as â€œBuffels-hoornâ€ (not
â€œBuffelsdoornâ€), on account of the horn-like calyx lobes,
which persist on the fruit. The bright-red flowers give rise to the
name â€œWild pomegranate,â€ or â€œWilde granaat.â€ There
are also various native names for the plant.

The single species of this genus is endemic to South Africa,
and has a wide distribution. In the south-west it is known as far
as Swellendam, whence it ranges through the forests to Natal and
the Transvaal. Mr. Galpin has recorded the plant from the summit
of Saddleback Mountain, at 4500 to 5000 ft., where it occurs as
a shrub 8 ft. high. It is somewhat variable, the corolla differing
much in size, and the length and hairiness of the style fluctuates,
perhaps due to sexual differences. The calyx lobes are either 5 or
6 on the same plant.

No less than six different names have been applied to this
species. Of these we have, with some reluctance, adopted the
oldest, *B. bubalina*, Sims, using the specific name first applied

by the younger Linnaeus in 1781 under the genus *Lonicera* for specimens collected by Sparmann. A better known name is *B. capensis.*

DESCRIPTION:—A small tree reaching 3Â·6 to 4Â·2 m. high. *Leaves* opposite, petiolate; petioles up to 1Â·2 cm. long, thick, pubescent; lamina up to 10Â·5 cm. long and 5Â·5 cm. broad, broadly ovate, entire, rounded or subcordate at the base, with revolute margins and the veins conspicuous above and very prominent beneath, dark green and glabrous above, pubescent on all the veins beneath. *Stipules* semicircular from a broad base, ending in a linear cusp which almost equals the basal portion in length and is minutely pilose. *Inflorescence* terminal, many-flowered. *Calyx-tube* 6 mm. long, campanulate; lobes 5 to 6, 1 to 2 cm. long, linear, pubescent. *Corolla-tube* 2 cm. long, inflated, puberulous without, glabrous within, with a ring of white hairs near the base; lobes 5 mm. long, triangular. *Stamens* 5, inserted on the upper half of the corolla-tube; filaments very short; anthers with the connective slightly produced. *Ovary* inferior, 2-celled, many-ovuled; style filiform, exserted; stigma clavate. *Fruit* a subglobose berry, crowned with the persistent calyx-lobes.

PLATE 145.—Fig. 1, calyx; Fig. 2, corolla laid open; Fig. 3, show-ing pistil in calyx; Fig. 4, anther; Fig. 5, cross-section of ovary; Fig. 6, stipule.

F.P.S.A., 1924.

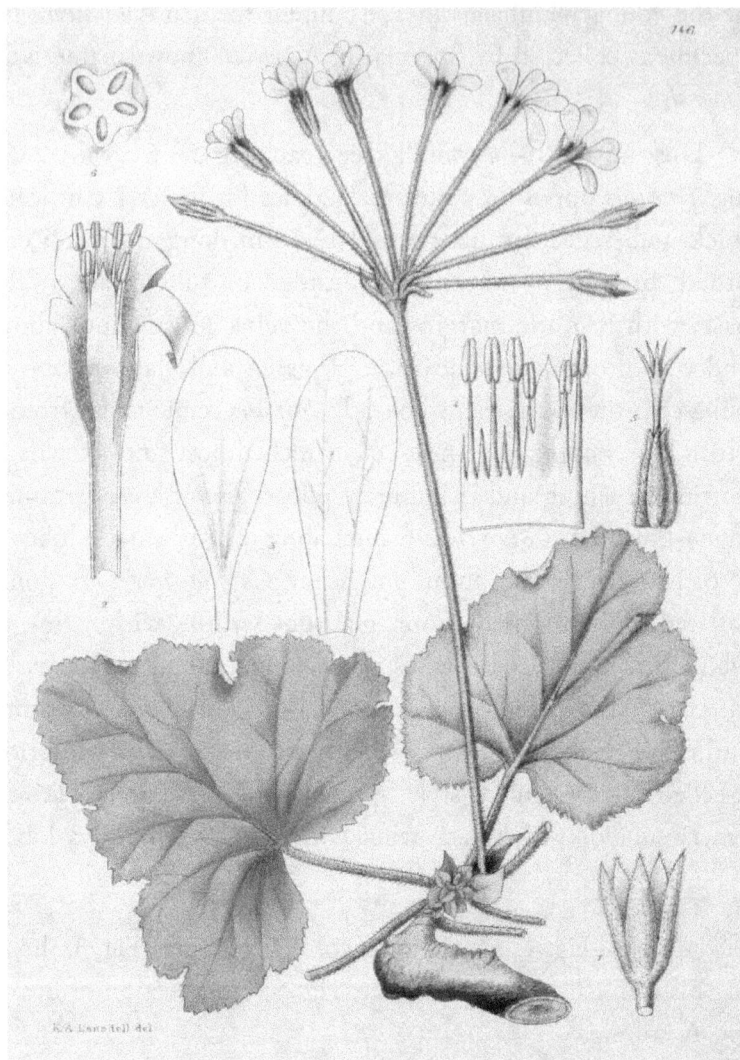

PLATE 146.

PELARGONIUM PULVERULENTUM.
Cape Province, Natal.

GERANIACEAE. *Tribe* PELARGONIEAE.

PELARGONIUM, *Lâ€™Herit.*; *Benth. et Hook. f. Gen. Plant.*
Pelargonium pulverulentum, *Colv. in Sw. Ger. t. 218; Fl.*

THIS species of *Pelargonium*, according to the late Dr. J. Medley Wood, was first found in Natal in 1878, and was not met with again until 1914, when it was found on the south coast near the sea. It had previously been recorded from the eastern districts of the Cape Province by Ecklon and Zeyher, DrÄ¨ge and Burke. The species belongs to the section *Polyactium* of the genus, and should be compared with *Pelargonium crassicaule*, which we figured on Plate 52.

The white powdery pubescence, mentioned by Sweet as covering the young leaves, has not been noticed in the Natal plants.

Our illustration was made and the description drawn up from specimens collected at Merebank, Natal.

DESCRIPTION:—*Stem* short, thick, woody. *Leaves* petioled; petioles 3Â·1 to 7Â·5 cm. long, hispid; lamina 6Â·5 to 8Â·1 cm. long and broad, cordate, obtuse, somewhat lobed, with the lobes rounded and irregularly and sharply serrate, 5-veined at the base, glabrous above, hispid with minute short hairs beneath, more thickly on the margins; stipules broadly ovate, acute, ciliate. *Inflo-*

rescence an umbel of 6 to 12 flowers. *Peduncle* up to 20 cm. long, hispid. *Bracts* 3 to 4Â·5 cm. long, oblong, acute, hispid, ciliate. *Sepals* 5, oblong-lanceolate, acute, densely and minutely hispid, shorter than the petals. *Petals* 5, rather unequal, 1 to 1Â·2 cm. long, obovate, yellowish-white with a purple blotch. *Stamens* 10, monadelphous, unequal; 6 stamens fertile; the remainder without anthers, of these 3 are short and subulate and 1 broad and acute. *Stigmas* 5, filiform. Fruit not seen.

PLATE 146.—Fig. 1, calyx; Fig. 2, longitudinal section of the flower showing the monadelphous stamens; Fig. 3, petals; Fig. 4, stamens; Fig. 5, pistil; Fig. 6, cross-section through the ovary.

F.P.S.A., 1924.

PLATE 147.

ACANTHACEAE. *Tribe* THUNBERGIEAE.

THUNBERGIA, *Linn.*; *Benth. et Hook. f. Gen. Plant.*
Thunbergia natalensis, *Hook. Bot. Mag. t. 5082; Fl.*

Thunbergia natalensis was described and figured in 1858 from plants cultivated by Messrs. Veitch of Chelsea, from seed received from South Africa. A year later Harvey gave a picture of the species in his *Thesaurus Capensis* (Plate 38). The *Flora Capensis* does not mention the peculiar stalked glandular hairs found on the funnel-shaped part of the style, though Hooker accurately figured these, neither does Harvey show them in his figure nor mention them in his description, although he was acquainted with the drawing in the *Botanical Magazine*.

The plant is a small shrub bearing large blue flowers with a bright yellow throat, and is confined to the eastern parts of the Cape Province, Natal, and the spurs of the Drakensbergen in the Transvaal. Notwithstanding its showy nature, it escaped the notice of the old collectors in Natal and the Transkei.

The species is worth the attention of horticulturists, and should find greater favour among growers who cultivate our native plants.

DESCRIPTION:—A shrub 20 to 50 cm. high. *Branches* glabrous or thinly hairy. *Leaves* 4 to 9 cm. long, 4 to 7 cm. broad, decussate, oblong or elliptic, acute, cordate or sub-hastate at the base, subentire or sinuate-toothed, slightly scabrous on both surfaces, with the veins prominent beneath; petiole 3 to 6 mm. long. *Inflorescence* axillary 1-to 3-flowered; bracteoles 2, 1 to 2Â·5 cm. long, 1 to 1Â·3 cm. broad, lanceolate, acute, prominently 3-veined; peduncle 2 to 4 cm. long, glabrous. *Calyx-tube* 2 mm. long; lobes ovate. *Corolla* salver-shaped; tube 2 to 3Â·5 cm. long, curved, much inflated from near the base, sparsely pubescent; lobes 1 to 1Â·3 cm. long, ovate. *Stamens* inserted on the corolla-tube; filaments filiform, thickened towards the base; anther-cells bearded, one cell in each of the two larger anthers spurred at the base. *Style* funnel-shaped above, and produced in short triangular lobes, with stalked glandular-hairs on the funnel-shaped part and bearded on the lower surface of the lobes. *Capsule* 3 cm. long, densely and minutely hairy or glabrous.

PLATE 147.—Fig. 1, showing ovary situated on the disc; Fig. 2, stamen; Fig. 3, portion of style, showing funnel-shaped upper portion covered with stalked glandular hairs; Fig. 4, fruit.

F.P.S.A., 1924.

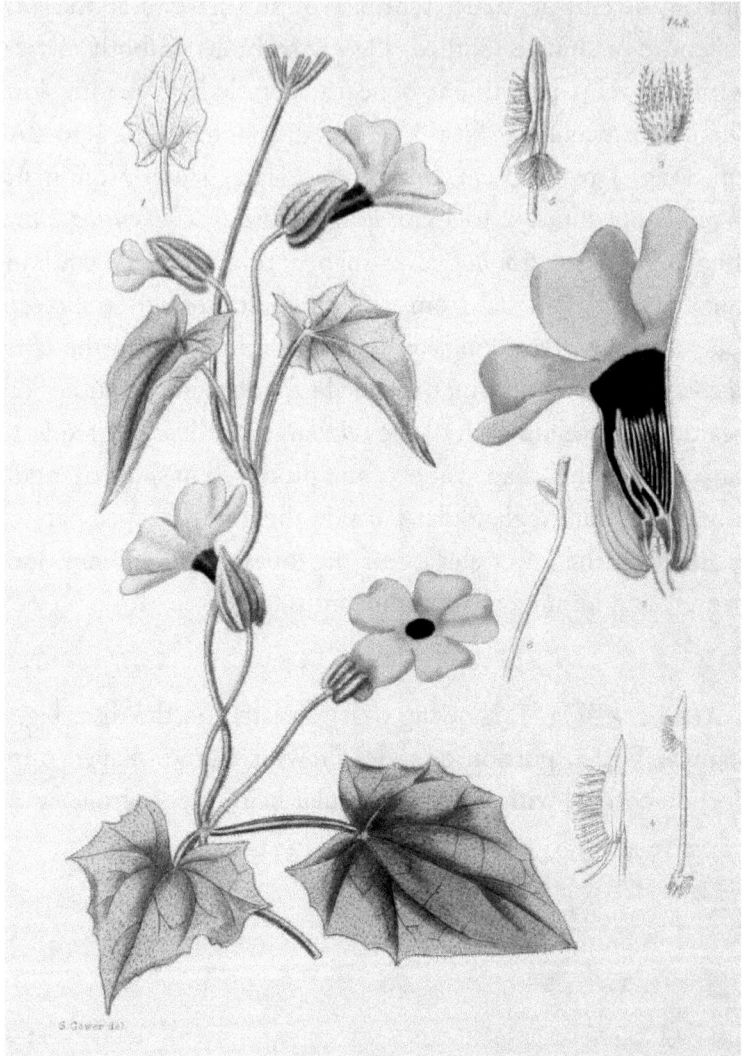

PLATE 148.

THUNBERGIA ALATA.

Natal.

ACANTHACEAE. *Tribe* THUNBERGIEAE.

THUNBERGIA, *Linn. fil.; Benth. et Hook. f. Gen. Plant.*

Thunbergia alata, *Boj. ex Sims in Bot. Mag. t. 2591; Fl.*

Thunbergia alata is a native of tropical Africa and Natal, but has been introduced into many warm parts of the world as an ornamental creeper, and it is often called â€œBlack-eyed Susan.â€ It was first described and figured in 1825 from plants raised in England from seed collected in Mauritius.

In its natural habitat the species is found as a creeper in woods, and the bright-orange corolla with a dark maroon throat gives the flower a singularly beautiful effect. The plant grows readily under cultivation, and makes a fine trellis creeper, but in colder countries it requires the protection of a glass-house.

The petioles of the mature leaves, as will be seen from the plate, are distinctly winged, but in the younger leaves they are almost terete. The stamens, as is usually the case in the family *Acanthaceae*, are appendaged in some way, and exhibit two forms in this species. All the anthers are tailed, but the anther of the shorter stamen, instead of having two tails, is only tailed at the base of one pollen-sac, the other pollen-sac bearing a bunch of radiating glandular hairs.

Our plate was prepared from plants grown by Dr. I. B. Pole Evans, C.M.G., at Irene, near Pretoria.

DESCRIPTION:—A climber. *Branches* terete, hirsute. *Leaves* opposite, petioled; petiole 2 to 5 cm. long, at first terete, with a shallow groove on the upper side, at length expanded and winged, hirsute; lamina 2Â·2 to 6Â·5 cm. long, 2 to 5Â·5 cm. broad, ovate, subobtuse, lobed at the base, hirsute above and beneath, with the veins depressed above, prominent beneath. *Flowers* solitary, axillary. *Pedicel* up to 6 cm. long, terete, hirsute. *Bracts* two, 2Â·2 cm. long, 1Â·2 cm. broad, ovate, obtuse, distinctly keeled, hirsute, connate on one side. *Calyx* with many narrow linear lobes, covered with stalked glands. *Corolla-tube* 2 cm. long, cylindric below, and then more or less suddenly widened into a tube 6 mm. in diameter above, glabrous without and with a ring of deflexed glandular hairs at the insertion of the stamens; limb more or less oblique, with the lobes 1Â·5 cm. long, 1Â·4 cm. broad, obovate, and with the margin concave at the apex. *Stamens* unequal; anthers very distinctly tailed and covered on the face with long glandular hairs; the shorter anther with only 1 tail and with a tuft of glandular hairs on the other pollen sac. *Style-lobes* unequal; the shorter in the form of a concave saucer; the upper deeply channelled (*National Herb. Pretoria*, No. 2847).

PLATE 148.—Fig. 1, young leaf with terete petiole; Fig. 2, median longitudinal section of flower; Fig. 3, calyx; Fig. 4, larger stamens; Fig. 5, smaller stamen; Fig. 6, style.

F.P.S.A., 1924.

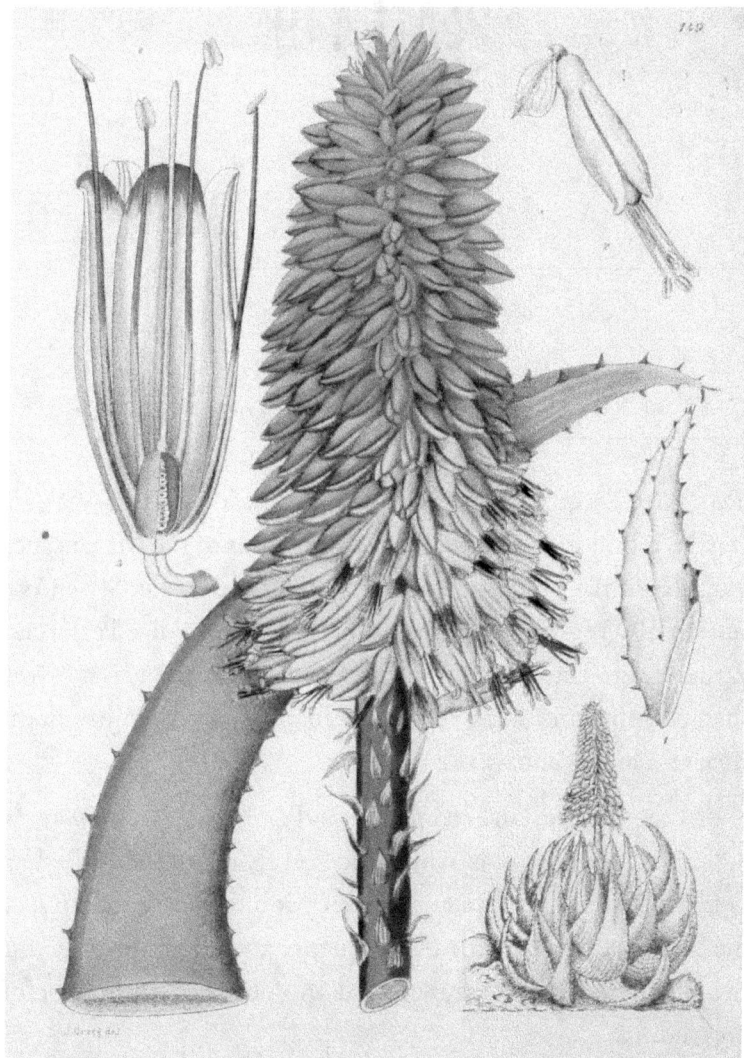

PLATE 149.

ALOE PEGLERAE.

Transvaal.

LILIACEAE. *Tribe* ALOINEAE.

ALOE, *Linn.*; *Benth. et Hook. f. Gen. Plant.*

Aloe Peglerae, *Schonl. in Records Albany Mus.*

Aloe Peglerae is quite a common plant in parts of the Transvaal, and may be found in quantities on the stony hills of the Magaliesberg round Pretoria. The species was first described by Dr. S. SchÄ¶nland in 1903 from specimens collected by Miss Alice Pegler near Rustenburg. The peculiar lax arrangement of the leaves is very characteristic, and Miss Pegler not inaptly compared its appearance to a loose cabbage.

In the description accompanying Plate 107 (*Aloe comosa*) we described the method in which the flowers mature. *Aloe Peglerae*, as far as we have observed, is an exception to this general rule, as the style is exserted with the filaments and does not wait until the filaments are withdrawn, and the perianth withers before protruding.

Our plate was prepared from specimens which flowered at the Division of Botany, Pretoria.

DESCRIPTION:—*Plant* almost acaulescent with a dense rosette of leaves. *Leaves* curved, about 28 cm. long, 5Â·5 cm. broad, below lanceolate, ending in a short spine, almost flat on the upper surface, slightly convex on the lower surface, faintly keeled and spiny on the back in the uppermost third, with the margins spiny; the spines on lower portion of leaf about 1 mm. long and about 5 mm. apart, becoming 5 mm. long and 1Â·5 cm. apart in the upper part of the leaf. *Peduncle* solitary from the middle of the leaf rosette, about 1Â·2 cm. in diameter and covered with ovate long-acuminate erect membranous bracts. *Flower spike* about 18 cm. long, up to 8 cm. in diameter; flowers at first reddish, becoming greenish-white at maturity. *Outer perianth-segments* 2Â·5 cm. long, 6 mm. broad, oblanceolate, with the apex slightly recurved, 3-nerved; inner segments 2 cm. long, 8 mm. broad, oblong, 1-nerved. *Stamens* at length long exserted; filaments dark purple above, greenish below, linear. *Ovary* 5 mm. long, ellipsoid; style 4Â·2 cm. long, cylindric, exserted with the stamens; stigma small (*National Herb. Pretoria*, No. 2846).

PLATE 149.—Fig. 1, upper portion of leaf; Fig. 2, flower; Fig. 3, median longitudinal section of a flower.

F.P.S.A., 1924.

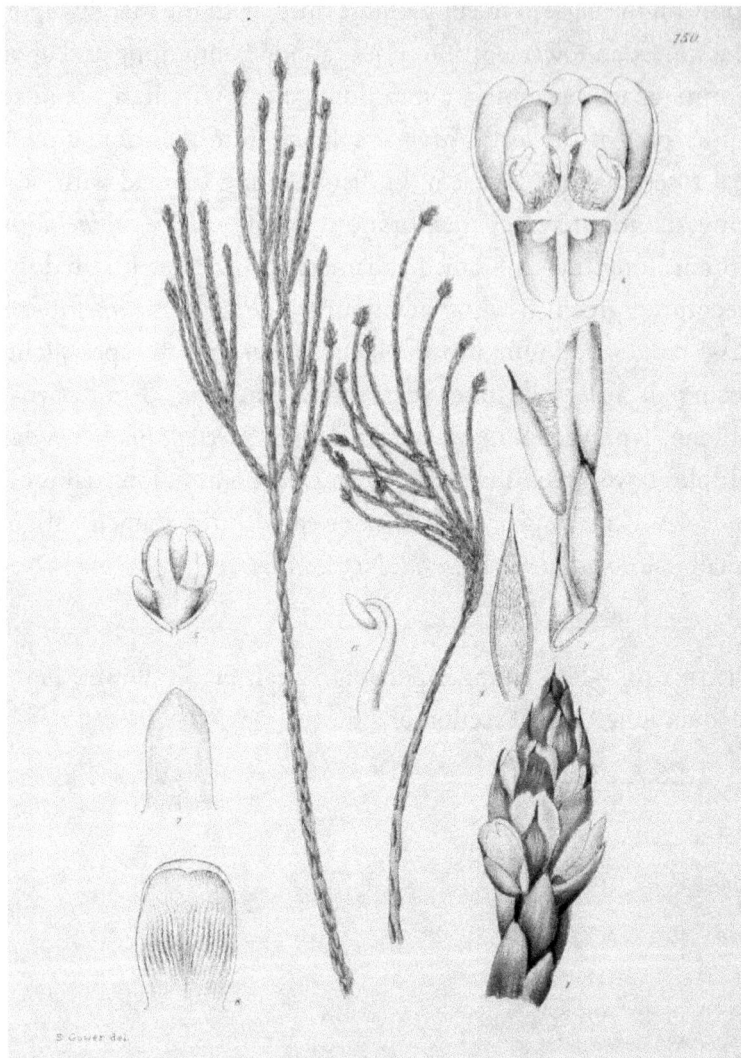

PLATE 150.

PSEUDOBAECKEA VIRGATA.

Cape Province.

BRUNIACEAE.

PSEUDOBAECKIA, *Nied. in Engl. and Prantl. Naturl. Pflanzenfam.*
Pseudobaeckia virgata, *Nied. l. c.*; *Dummer in Journ.*
Bot. 1912, Suppl. 2. *Brunia virgata*, Brogn.; *Fl.*

ON Plate 92 we figured a member of the family *Bruniaceae, Brunia Stokoei,* which differs from the genus *Pseudobaeckia* in having the sepals united beyond the ovary and the stamens shorter than the petals. The species of *Pseudobaeckia* were formerly placed under the genus *Brunia,* until a separate genus was constituted for them in 1891.

The species figured is not a particularly striking one, but it is worthy of illustration, as it belongs to a group only found in the south-western area of the Cape Province.

The specimens from which our plate was prepared were collected by Mr. T. P. Stokoe on the Hottentot Hollands Mountains, where it is found growing in very damp places near Kogelberg. It also occurs in the mountains of Swellendam. We are indebted to the Director of the Royal Botanic Gardens, Kew, for comparing the plant with the material in the Kew Herbarium.

DESCRIPTION:—*Branches* slender, arranged in a racemose manner above, yellowish, the young branches densely woolly, at length becoming glabrous. *Leaves* adpressed, somewhat distant below, becoming more crowded above, 3Â·5 to 6 mm. long, 1Â·5 mm. broad, lanceolate, with a long black mucro at the apex, convex and glabrous beneath, concave and woolly above. *Flowers* sessile, solitary in the uppermost leaves of the ultimate branchlets. *Bracts* two, 1 mm. long, Â·25 mm. broad, linear, convex beneath, concave above, obtuse, glabrous. *Sepals* 1Â·25 mm. long, Â·5 mm. broad, oblong, obtuse, glabrous. *Petals* 1 mm. long, slightly over Â·5 mm. broad, oblong, obtuse. *Filaments* Â·5 mm. long, linear; anthers less than Â·25 mm. long. *Ovary* 2-celled, with a single red pendulous ovule in each cell, sometimes only one ovule present; style Â·5 mm. long, bifid at the apex (*National Herb. Pretoria*, No. 2578).

PLATE 150.—Fig. 1, tip of branch enlarged, showing flowers; Fig. 2, portion of branch enlarged; Fig. 3, single leaf showing under surface; Fig. 4, longitudinal section through a flower; Fig. 5, a single flower; Fig. 6, stamen; Fig. 7, bracteole; Fig. 8, bract.

F.P.S.A., 1924.

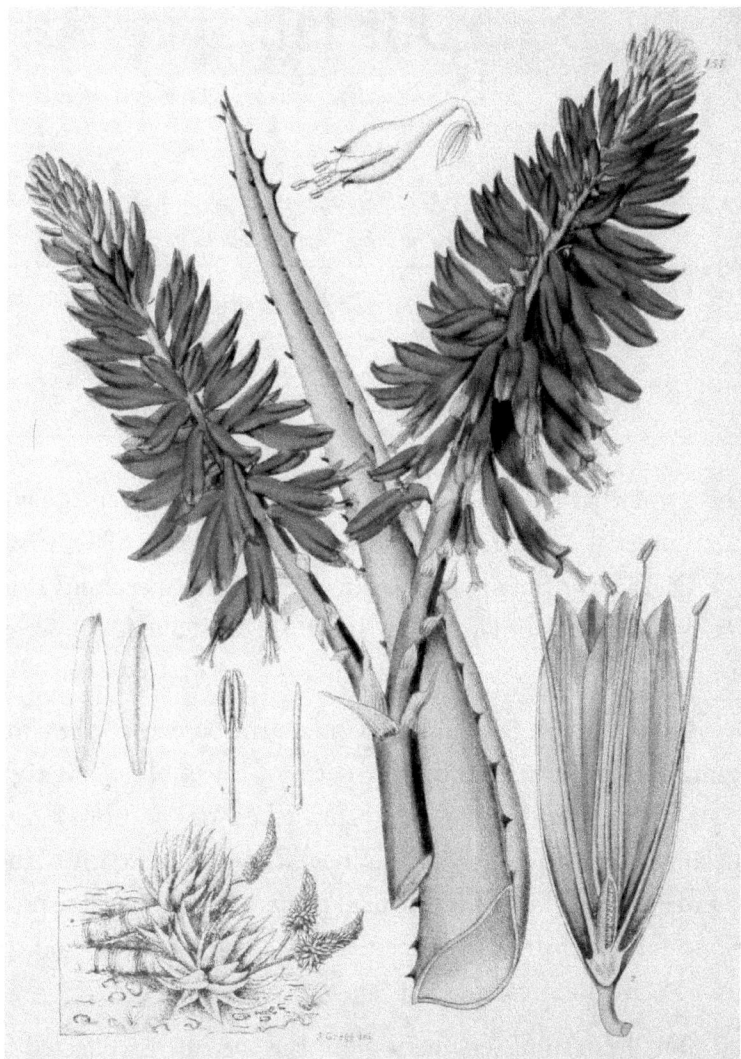

PLATE 151.

ALOE SCHLECHTERI.
Cape Province, Namaqualand.

LILIACEAE. *Tribe* ALOINEAE.

ALOE, *Linn.*; *Benth. et Hook. f. Gen. Plant.*
Aloe Schlechteri, *Schonl. in Records Albany Mus.*

This somewhat rare *Aloe* was first described by Dr. Schönland from material collected by Max Schlechter at Pella, S.W. Africa. The Division of Botany in 1921 received living specimens from Dr. W. Borchards of Upington, and these subsequently flowered at Pretoria.

Aloe Schlechteri is found growing on the bare veld. The short stems are decumbent and the rosette of leaves almost at right angles to the stems, giving the plant, when viewed from a little distance, an acaulescent appearance. The plants are invariably found in groups, and the individual plants are so arranged that the group forms a half-circle or sometimes a complete circle on the ground. The inflorescence appears to be always forked.

Our illustration was made from the specimens collected by Dr. Borchards.

DESCRIPTION:—*Stem* short decumbent with a dense rosette of leaves. *Leaves* somewhat incurved, up to 24 cm. long, up to 4 cm. broad near the base, lanceolate, acuminate, ending in a sharp spine, convex beneath, flat or slightly convex above, with the margins covered with prickles and a few prickles on the keel beneath near the apex; prickles about 1Â·2 cm. apart, straight or slightly incurved. *Inflorescence* branched into two arms; the common peduncle about 10 cm. long, bluntly 3-angled, naked; peduncle of arms up to lowermost flowers 9 cm. long, covered with a few membranous ovate acuminate bracts; raceme 15 cm. long, many-flowered. *Pedicels* 8 mm. long, erect. *Youngest flowers* tubular, erect, becoming later horizontal and at length pendulous and then clavate. *Perianth-tube* 1Â·8 cm. long, widening from the base upwards; inner lobes 1Â·2 cm. long, 8 mm. broad, lanceolate, obtuse, usually 5-nerved; outer lobes 1Â·6 cm. long, 8 mm. broad, oblong-lanceolate, obtuse, concave usually 3-nerved. *Stamens* 3Â·5 cm. long, at first included, at length exserted. *Ovary* 8 mm. long, 3-angled; style 1Â·6 cm. long, terete; stigma minute (National Herb. 2845).

PLATE 151.—Fig. 1, flower; Fig. 2, median longitudinal section of flower; Fig. 3, perianth-segments; Fig. 4, stamen; Fig. 5, style.

F.P.S.A., 1924.

PLATE 152.

MONTBRETIA CROCOSMAEFLORA.

Transvaal.

IRIDACEAE. Tribe IXIEAE.

Montbretia crocosmaeflora, *Hort.; Flor. Mag. n.s. t. 472; Fl.*

This plant, commonly seen in South African gardens, is a hybrid between *Tritonia Pottsii* and *Crocosmia aurea*, and was described from plants which flowered at the Royal Botanic Gardens, Kew, in August 1889. As the plant has been described under the generic name of *Montbretia* in the *Flora Capensis* we retain the combination here.

The plant blooms in Pretoria during the month of April, and furnishes a good supply of cut flowers during a time when they are scarce. Our illustration was made from specimens flowering at the Division of Botany, Pretoria.

DESCRIPTION:—*Corm* 2Â·5 cm. in diameter, almost spherical, sending out lateral rhizomes. *Leaves* arranged up the stem in a fan-like manner, 6 to 7 on each side, up to 30 cm. long, Â·8 to 1 cm. broad, linear, acute, equitant at the base, with the midrib prominent and the lateral veins evident in fresh specimens, glabrous. *Peduncle* up to 25 cm. long, 7-to 10-ribbed (almost narrowly winged), glabrous. *Inflorescence* a lax panicle of 3 to 4 spikes. *Spikes* 4 to 5 cm. long, 4-to 6-flowered. *Spathe-valves* 8 mm. long, ovate, acuminate, brown, membranous. *Perianth-tube* 1Â·5 cm. long, 4 mm. in diameter above, gradually narrowing below;

lobes 2Â·8 cm. long, 9 mm. broad, oblong, obtuse, somewhat unequal. *Stamens* fixed in the upper portion of the perianth-tube; filaments 2Â·2 mm. long, terete; anthers 8 mm. long, linear, versatile. *Ovary* 6 mm. long, ellipsoid; style 3 cm. long, terete; style-branches 1 mm. long, bifid and papillose at the apex. *Fruit* 9 mm. in diameter, globose, obtusely 3-angled, several seeds in each cell (National Herb. 2848).

PLATE 152.—Fig. 1, corm showing rhizomes; Fig. 2, median longitudinal section of a flower; Fig. 3, spathe-valves; Fig. 4, stamen; Fig. 5, upper part of style; Fig. 6, fruits.

F.P.S.A., 1924.

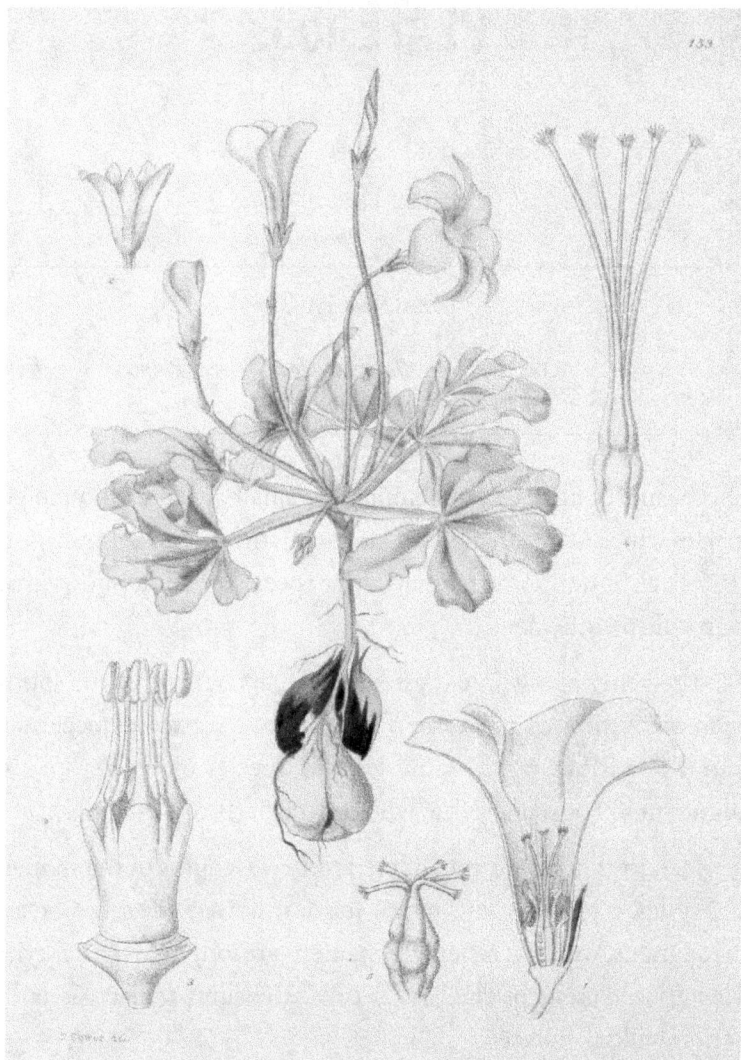

PLATE 153.

OXALIS LUPINIFOLIUS.
Cape Province.

OXALIDACEAE.

OXALIS, *Linn.*; *Benth. et Hook. f. Gen. Plant.*
Oxalis lupinifolius, *Jacq. Oxal. t. 72; Fl.*

This beautiful little *Oxalis* belongs to a small group of about eight species which are characterised by having the leaves digitately 5-to 19-foliate, and in some respects these species are more showy than many of the others.

The genus as a whole is essentially characteristic of the south-western portion of the Cape Province, but scattered species are found in various parts of the Union. Species of *Oxalis* are also abundant in South America, where some of them form tall shrubs.

Heterostylism, *i. e.* the different relative lengths of the stamens and styles, is found in the genus. In some flowers the styles exceed the stamens, while in others the stamens are longer than the styles. This arrangement of the sexual organs ensures that cross-pollination will take place.

Our plate was prepared from specimens grown at the Division of Botany, Pretoria, from corms presented by Dr. C. L. Leipoldt, who collected them at Pakhuis in the Clanwilliam Division. According to Dr. Leipoldt the corms are edible.

DESCRIPTION:—Internodes very short, so that the leaves appear more or less in a rosette. *Leaves* digitately 3-to 6-foliate;

petioles 3 to 9 cm. long, 4 to 5 mm. broad, flattened glabrous; the shorter petioles very distinctly winged; the longer petioles not so evidently winged; leaflets up to 3Â·5 cm. long, 1Â·8 cm. broad, obovate, cuneate, rounded at the apex, glabrous, punctate beneath. *Pedicels* 1 to 6 cm. long, terete, glabrous. *Bracts* 2, 4 mm. long, linear. *Sepals* 6 mm. long, 2 mm. broad, oblong, obtuse, with membranous margins, glabrous. *Corolla-tube* 7 mm. long, 5 mm. in diameter above, campanulate; lobes 1Â·5 cm. long, 1 cm. broad, obovate. *Stamens* unequal; longer stamens 6Â·5 mm. long, subterete, pubescent, with an appendage on the back; shorter stamens 3Â·5 mm. long, similar to the longer, but without the appendage; anthers oblong. *Ovary* 1Â·5 mm. long, 1 mm. in diameter, ellipsoid, glabrous; styles 1 mm. long; stigmas penicillate.

PLATE 153.—Fig. 1, median longitudinal section of flower; Fig. 2, calyx; Fig. 3, androecium; Fig. 4, pistil of long-styled flower; Fig. 5. pistil of short-styled flower.

F.P.S.A., 1924.

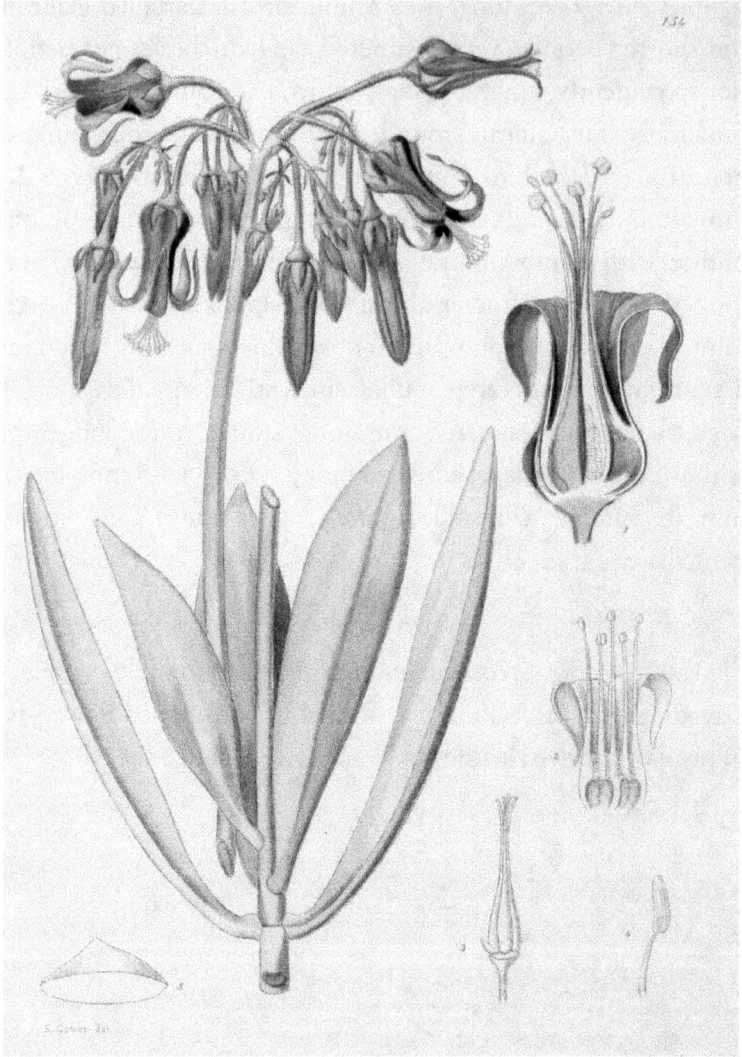

PLATE 154.

COTYLEDON Wickensii.

Transvaal.

CRASSULACEAE.

COTYLEDON, *Linn.*; *Benth. et Hook. f. Gen. Plant.*

Cotyledon Wickensii, *Schonl. in Records Albany Museum.*

The *Pillansii* group of *Cotyledon* as defined by Dr. SchÃ¶nland includes species with a suffructicose, mostly robust habit, with the lobes of the corolla usually longer than the tube, glandular flowers, and with a tuft of hairs at the base of the filaments where they join the corolla. The species figured here was collected by Mr. J. Wickens and Dr. I. B. Pole Evans, C.M.G., on stony kopjes at Smitâ€™s Drift, in the Pietersburg District of the northern Transvaal.

It is well adapted for rockeries, and flowers profusely during the mid-winter months of June and July. The species has been established in the rockeries of the Union Building gardens at Pretoria, and is doing remarkably well.

Our plate was prepared from specimens growing at the Division of Botany, Pretoria.

DESCRIPTION:—A tall herbaceous shrub up to 2 m. high. *Stems* somewhat fleshy, glabrous. *Leaves* 8Â·5 to 11 cm. long, 2Â·5 cm. broad, lanceolate, acute, or sometimes rounded, distinctly narrowed to the base into a terete portion, flat above, slightly convex beneath, glabrous and covered with a glaucous bloom. *Inflorescence* cymose, 12-to 15-flowered at the end of a naked peduncle. *Peduncle* up to 30 cm. long, terete, 6 mm. in diameter. *Pedicels* 1Â·5 to 3 cm. long, terete, densely covered with glandular hairs, expanded and disc-like above. *Sepals* 8 mm. long, 4 mm. broad, ovate, obtuse, glandular-pubescent. *Petals* persistent. *Corolla-tube* 2 mm. long, gibbous at the base between the petals, glandular hispid; lobes 2 cm. long, 2 mm. broad, oblong-linear, with a small blunt apiculus, glandular-hispid, especially on the margins. *Stamens* equal; filaments 2Â·2 cm. long, terete, with reflexed hairs at the base; anthers ovate or almost orbicular. *Carpels* a little shorter than the stamens. *Glands* at base of each carpel, 3 mm. long, 1Â·5 mm. broad, oblong, truncate, projecting into the cavity at base of the petals.

PLATE 154.—Fig. 1, median longitudinal section of flower; Fig. 2, longitudinal section of flower with pistil removed; Fig. 3, carpels showing glands at the base; Fig. 4, stamen; Fig. 5, cross-section of leaf.

F.P.S.A., 1924.

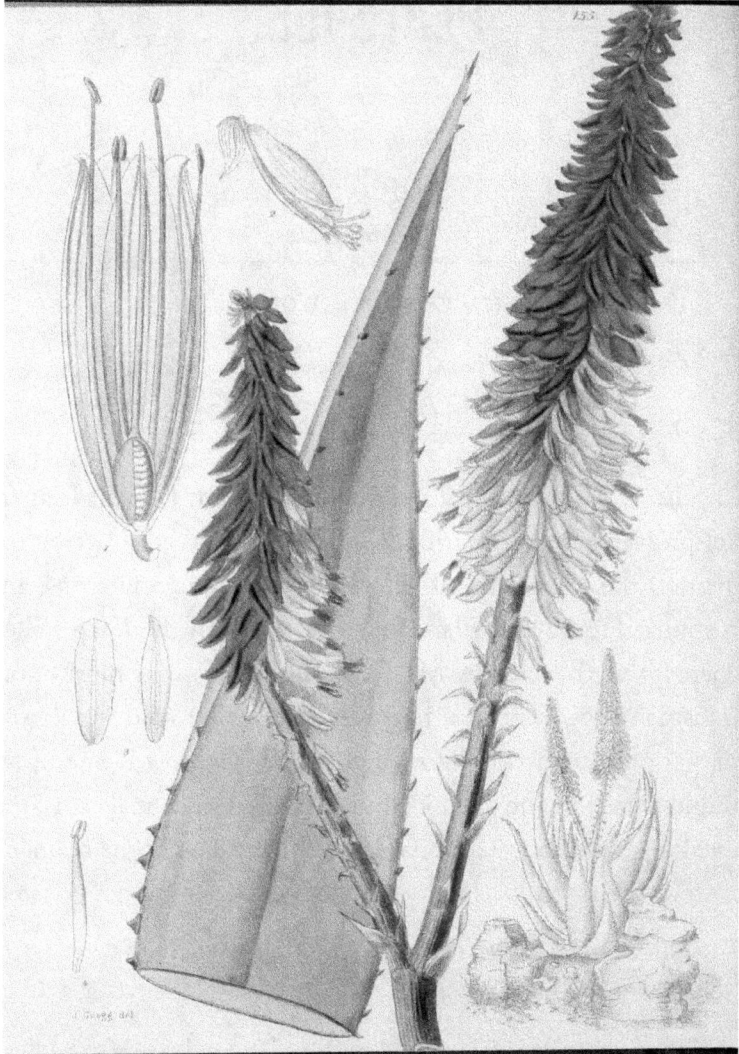

PLATE 155.

ALOE PETRICOLA.

Transvaal.

Liliaceae. *Tribe* Aloineae.

Aloe, *Linn.*; *Benth. et Hook. f. Gen. Plant.*

Aloe petricola, *Pole Evans in Trans. Roy. Soc. S. Afr.*

This *Aloe* was first collected and photographed by Dr. Pole Evans at Nelspruit in September 1905. In the Nelspruit Valley (Barberton District) the plant is found chiefly on the granite outcrops, and in similar localities at Elandâ€™s Hoek and in the Kaap Valley, where it was collected by Mr. Geo. Thorncroft. Like most of our Transvaal aloes, it flowers in mid-winter (July), and the flowering period extends well into August. *Aloe petricola* is one of the stemless species, and the bicoloured inflorescence makes it quite a striking plant in the rockery. In the oldest flowers the filaments contract within the perianth, and the style then becomes exserted.

Our plate was prepared from specimens which flowered at the Division of Botany, Pretoria.

Description:—*Leaves* 34 cm. long, 8 cm. broad at the base, lanceolate, acuminate, ending in a short spine, concave on the upper surface, convex on the lower, with spines along the margins and 1 to 3 spines on the back near the apex; spines about Â·2 mm. long and 1Â·5 cm. apart. *Inflorescence* forked; peduncle bearing the inflorescence about 20 cm. long, 1Â·2 cm. in diameter, terete, bearing ovate acuminate membranous bracts; flowers in a dense spike about 21 cm. long, 6 cm. in diameter, all reflexed, at first red, later becoming greenish-white, with dark green bands. *Floral bracts* membranous, reflexed, 1Â·5 cm. long, 5 mm. broad at the base, ovate, cuspidate, 5-nerved. *Outer perianth-segments* 2Â·5 cm. long, 6 mm. broad, lanceolate, obtuse, distinctly 3-nerved (faintly 5-nerved); inner segments 2Â·3 cm. long, 9 mm. broad, somewhat keeled, 3-nerved. *Filaments* 2Â·5 cm. long, broadest in the middle and tapering to the base and apex, dark purple above, greenish-white below; anthers 3 mm. long with dark yellow pollen. *Ovary* 5 mm. long, cylindric; style 2 cm. long, cylindric; stigma minute.

PLATE 155.—Fig. 1, median longitudinal section of flower; Fig. 2, bud; Fig. 3, perianth-segments; Fig. 4, stamen.

F.P.S.A., 1924.

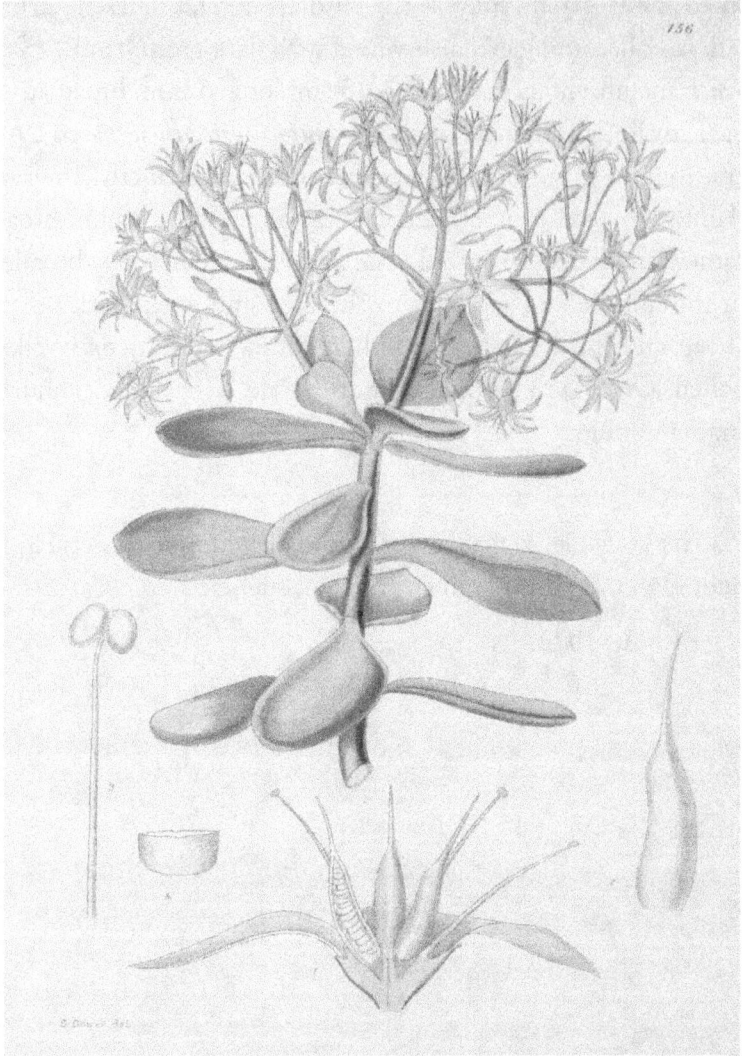

PLATE 156.

CRASSULA PORTULACEA.

Cape Province.

CRASSULACEAE.

CRASSULA, *Linn.; Benth. et Hook. f. Gen. Plant..*

Crassula portulacea, *Lam. Dict. ii. p. 172; Fl.*

This species of *Crassula* is somewhat related to *C. falcata*, figured on Plate 12, but differs in its more shrubby habit. It belongs to the section *Latifoliae* of the genus, which contains three species, all succulent branching shrubs, with broad flat fleshy leaves.

Crassula portulacea is a large much-branched shrub up to 10 to 12 ft. high, and is found in the south-eastern parts of the Cape Province, in the coastal districts from Montagu to Port Elizabeth.

Our plate was prepared from plants flowering in the rockeries at the Division of Botany, Pretoria. Here it forms a small, more or less compact shrub about 2 ft. high, and flowers very profusely. The flowers appear during the winter months, and when in full bloom the plant makes a very effective show on the rockery.

DESCRIPTION:—*Branches* succulent. *Leaves* up to 5 cm. long, 3 cm. broad, obovate, rounded at the apex, produced into a short broad petiole, articulated to the branches, glabrous. *Inflorescence* terminal, in large lax cymose panicles. *Calyx* campanulate, with very short lobes. *Petals* 1 cm. long, 2Â·5 mm. broad, oblong, with a small apiculus at the apex. *Stamens* 5, alternating with the petals; filaments 5Â·5 mm. long, linear, tapering upwards; anthers more or less crescent-shaped. *Hypogynous glands* oblong, rounded above. *Carpels* 5, free; ovary ellipsoid; style 3 mm. long, terete; stigma small, capitate.

PLATE 156.—Fig. 1, median longitudinal section of flower; Fig. 2, a single carpel; Fig. 3, stamen; Fig. 4, hypogynous gland.

F.P.S.A., 1924.

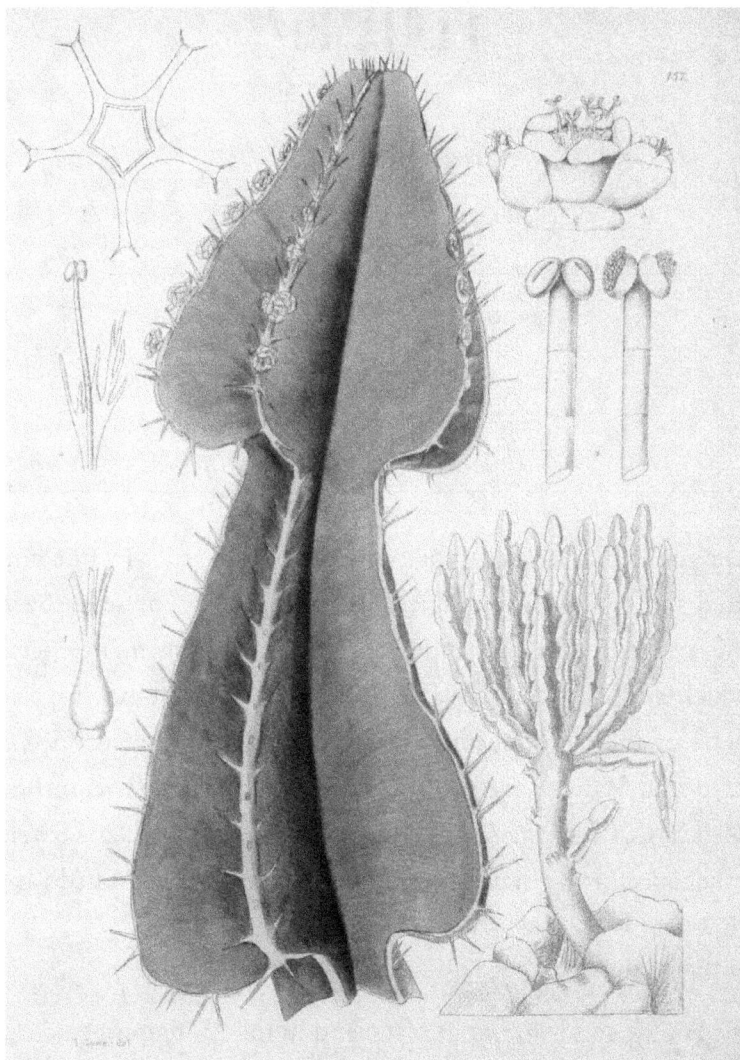

PLATE 157.

EUPHORBIA Cooperi.
Natal and Transvaal.

Euphorbiaceae. *Tribe* Euphorbieae.

Euphorbia, Linn.; Benth. et Hook. f. Gen. Plant.
Euphorbia Cooperi, *N.E. Br. ex Berger,*
Sukk. Euphorb. 83 and 84, Fig. 21;Fl.

The genus *Euphorbia* is represented in South Africa by one hundred and eighty-three species, and we figure a representative of this genus for the first time. The genus contains many species which are of economic value as stock-food plants in the drier parts of the country, and among these may be mentioned *E. esculenta*, Marl. (Vingerpol), *E. brachiata*, E. Mey. (Soet or Blou Melkbos), *E. coerulescens*, Haw. (Soet Noorsdoring), and several other species which are commonly known as â€œNoorsdoring. â€

The species figured here is one of the arborescent members of the family, and is found in Natal and in the Rustenburg and Piet Potgieterâ€™s Rust Districts of the Transvaal. It is easily recognised by the continuous horny margins on the stems.

The plant when cut exudes a copious milky juice, which is a skin irritant, and which also causes a burning sensation in the throat if the air is inhaled when standing in close proximity to a bleeding plant.

Our plate was prepared from a plant growing at the Division of Botany, Pretoria.

DESCRIPTION:—A succulent leafless spiny tree, 10 to 15 ft. high; trunk becoming naked and cylindric below, 15 to 20 cm. thick; branches ascending, curved at their basal part, 5-to 6-angled, deeply constricted into conic-ovate or somewhat heart-shaped segments 5 to 15 cm. long, and 4 to 7Â·5 cm. in diameter, with the small central solid part not more than 2 to 2Â·5 cm. thick in the younger branches, glabrous; angles wing-like, with triangular channels 2 to 4 cm. deep between them, their margins with a continuous horny nearly even grey border. *Leaves* rudimentary, scale-like, about 1 mm. long and 2 mm. broad, transverse, apiculate; spines 3 to 8 mm. long, in pairs 6 to 18 mm. apart, widely diverging, grey, with blackish tips; flowering-eyes 3 to 8 mm. above the spine-pairs; cymes 1 to 3 from the same eye, sessile, each with 3 involucres, glabrous. *Bracts* about 3 mm. long and 4 mm. broad, rounded, concave, usually minutely denticulate; involucres all sessile and the middle one male, lateral fertile, 5 to 6 mm. in diameter, cup-shaped, glabrous, with 5 glands and 5 erect short transversely rectangular fringed lobes; glands contiguous, 3 mm. in their greater diameter, narrowly transverse oblong, very minutely rugulose on the upper surface; capsule about 6 mm. long and 9 to 12 mm. in diameter, exserted on a stout pedicel, curved to one side, deeply 3-lobed seen from above, with laterally compressed lobes, glabrous, dark purple on the apex and along the angles, having a somewhat fleshy calyx at its base, with 3 deltoid-ovate acute lobes about 2 mm. long; cell-walls about 0Â·5 mm. thick, woody. *Styles* 2 mm. long, united for two-thirds of their length, with spreading arms, bifid at the apex; seeds 3 mm. in diameter, globose, with a raised line in a very slight furrow on one side, and a small pit at one end, light grey.

PLATE 157.—Fig. 1, cross section of stem; Fig. 2, inflorescence; Fig. 3, male flowers; Fig. 4, male flower with fringed lobe; Fig. 5, gynaecium of female flower.

F.P.S.A., 1924.

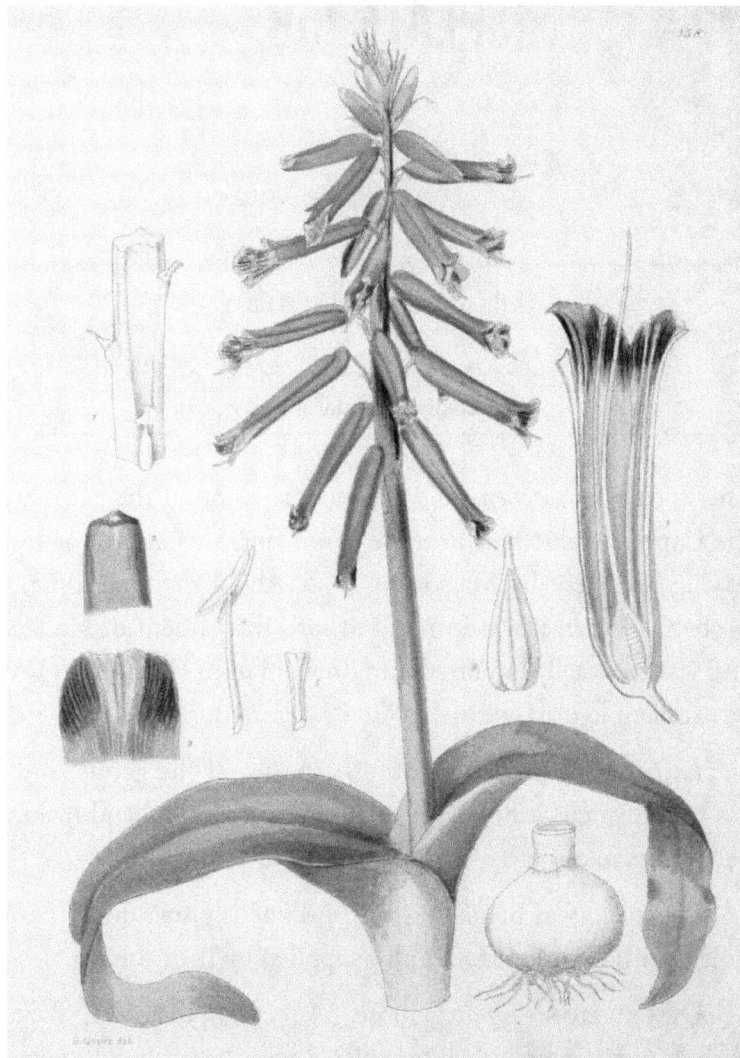

PLATE 158.

LACHENALIA PENDULA.
Cape Province.

LILIACEAE. *Tribe* SCILLEAE.

LACHENALIA, *Jacq.*; *Benth. et. Hook. f. Gen. Plant.*
Lachenalia pendula, *Ait. Hort. Kew.*

This species of *Lachenalia* was amongst some of the earliest of the Cape introductions into the Royal Botanic Gardens at Kew, having been sent by Masson in 1774. About the same time, or probably earlier, it was introduced into the gardens of Holland, and was eventually imported into England from Holland. In 1801 an excellent figure appeared in the *Botanical Magazine* (Plate 590).

Lachenalia pendula is a robust species of the genus, and is easily cultivated. It flowers freely under cultivation, and makes a very effective display.

Our plate was prepared from specimens grown by Dr. I. B. Pole Evans, C.M.G., from bulbs supplied by Lady Smartt.

DESCRIPTION:—*Bulb* globose, 3Â·5 cm. in diameter, covered with thin membranous white tunics. *Leaves* 2, clasping the base of the stem, up to 16 cm. long, up to 6 cm. broad below the middle, ovate, bluntly apiculate. *Peduncle* (including the flowers) up to 27 cm. long, 8 mm. in diameter, terete. *Bracts* small, broadly ovate, membranous. *Pedicels* 6 mm. long. *Flowers* arising from small pockets on the peduncle, first almost erect, then horizontal and at length pendulous. *Perianth-tube* slightly gibbous and oblique at the base; outer segments 3Â·3 cm. long, 7 mm. broad, oblong-linear, obtuse, with an outstanding ridge on the back near the apex, of one only; inner segments longer than the outer, 3Â·5 cm. long, 1 cm. broad near the apex, obovate-oblong, almost truncate at the apex. *Stamens* of two different lengths; the longer equalling the inner perianth-segments; the shorter slightly included; filaments terete, glabrous; anthers oblong. *Ovary* 5 mm. long, ellipsoid; style slightly exceeding the longer stamens, minutely capitate at the apex.

PLATE 158.—Fig. 1, median longitudinal section of a flower; Fig. 2, part of outer perianth-segment showing transverse ridge; Fig. 3, part of inner perianth-segment; Fig. 4, stamen; Fig. 5, upper portion of style; Fig. 6, ovary; Fig. 7, portion of peduncle with bracts and pockets from which the flowers arise.

F.P.S.A., 1924.

PLATE 159.

CYRTANTHUS GALPINI.
Transvaal.

AMARYLLIDACEAE. TRIBE AMARYLLEAE.

CYRTANTHUS, Ait.; Benth. et Hook. f. Gen. Plant.
Cyrtanthus Galpinii, *Baker in Kew Bull. 1892, Fl.*

We have pleasure in figuring for the first time this charming little *Cyrtanthus* from the Barberton District of the Transvaal. According to Mr. G. J. Hofmeyr, B.Sc., of the Forest Department, who collected the flowers, the plants are found growing in long grass at Kaapse Hoop. The plant is subsocial, and forms conspicuous pink patches in the veld. Mr. Hofmeyr informs us that the flowers at Barberton are scarlet, and not alizams pink (R. C. S), as in the Kaapse Hoop plants.

The species was first collected by Mr. E. E. Galpin, F.L.S., amongst rocks on Berea Ridge, near Barberton, in 1889. He describes the flowers as scarlet, dusted with gold. It flowers during the months of July and August.

C. Galpini falls into the same section of the genus as *C. helictus*, which we figured on Plate 99.

Our plate was partly prepared from Galpinâ€™s specimens (*Galpin* 409) and partly from living flowers collected by Mr. Hofmeyr.

DESCRIPTION:—*Bulb* ovoid, 2Â·5 to 3 mm. in diameter. *Leaves* appearing before the flowers, up to 8 cm. long, 2 mm. broad above, narrowing to a filiform portion below, with a single rib, glabrous. *Peduncle* 10 to 19 cm. long, 3 mm. in diameter, terete, very gradually narrowing upwards. *Bracts* 2Â·5 to 3 cm. long, scarious, linear, acuminate. *Flowers* solitary, more rarely 2-nate. *Perianth-tube* with a narrow-cylindric lower portion 1Â·5 cm. long, broadening out into a funnel-shaped portion 2 cm. long and 1Â·3 cm. in diameter at the throat; lobes 2 cm. long, 7 to 9 mm. broad, oblong, bluntly apiculate, with a very small tuft of glandular hairs on the apex of three of them. *Stamens* all arising from the base of the widened portion of the perianth-tube; filaments of unequal lengths and attached to the perianth-tube for different distances, giving the stamens the appearance of being in two rows; anthers oblong, versatile. *Ovary* 5 mm. long, ellipsoid; style 3-8 cm. long, filiform; stigmas 3 mm. long, recurved, papillose on the upper side.

PLATE 159.—Fig. 1, median longitudinal section of a flower; Fig. 2, portion of a perianth lobe showing apiculus and tuft of glandular hairs. Fig. 3, ovary.

F.P.S.A., 1924.

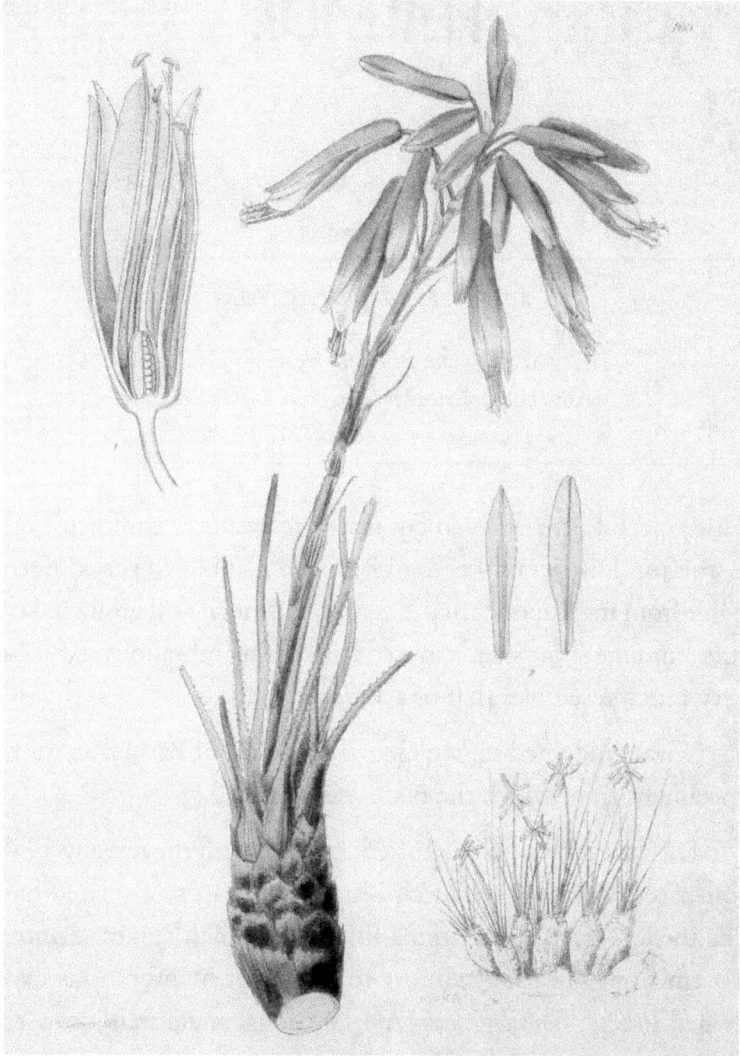

PLATE 160.

ALOE CHORTOLIRIOIDES.
Transvaal.

LILIACEAE. *Tribe* ALOINEAE.

ALOE, *Linn.*; *Benth. et Hook. f. Gen. Plant.*
Aloe chortolirioides, *Berger in Engl. Pflanzenreich,*
Liliac-Asphodel-Aloin. 171 (1908).

This graceful little *Aloe*, so far as we are aware, is confined to the Barberton District of the Transvaal. The plant has a very different habit from most species in the genus, inasmuch as it grows in large tufts, and the short stem, covered with the membranous leaf-bases, very much resembles that of a *Vellozia*.

We are indebted to Mr. Geo. Thorncroft of Barberton for the specimens from which the plate was prepared.

DESCRIPTION:—*Stems* tufted, covered with the remains of the leaf-bases; leaves 10 to 20 cm. long, linear from a dilated base, channelled, with the margins lined with small spines. *Peduncle* 16 cm. long, bearing, almost to the base, membranous ovate awned bracts. *Floral-bracts* 1Â·4 cm. long, membranous, ovate, long-acuminate, distinctly veined. *Pedicels* articulating at the apex and persistent. *Perianth* 3 cm. long, with a cylindric tube and 1-nerved lobes. *Stamens* exserted. *Style* 4 cm. long, filiform, long-exserted in old flowers (National Herb. 2733).

PLATE 160.—Fig. 1, median longitudinal section of flower; Fig. 2, perianth-segments.

F.P.S.A., 1924.

I. B. Pole Evans

INDEX TO VOLUME IV